THE INHERITANCE OF
HISTORIOGRAPHY
350–900

Edited by

Christopher Holdsworth and T.P. Wiseman

EXETER STUDIES IN HISTORY NO. 12

UNIVERSITY OF EXETER

First published 1986 by the University of Exeter

EXETER STUDIES IN HISTORY

General Editor: Colin Jones

Editorial Committee

B.J. Coles, BA MPhil FSA
M.D.D. Newitt, BA PhD FRHistS
M. Duffy, MA DPhil FRHistS
Professor I.A. Roots, MA FSA FRHistS

Publications

Exeter University Publications,
Hailey Wing,
Reed Hall,
Streatham Drive,
Exeter EX4 4QR

ISBN 0 85989 272 7
ISSN 0260 8628

Printed and Bound by A. Wheaton & Co. Ltd., Exeter

CONTENTS

NOTE ON CONTRIBUTORS

T.S. Brown is Lecturer in Mediæval History, University of Edinburgh.

Donald Bullough is Professor of Mediæval History, University of St Andrews.

Averil Cameron is Professor of Ancient History, King's College, University of London.

James Campbell is Fellow and Tutor in Modern History, Worcester College, Oxford.

Jill Harries is Lecturer in Ancient History, University of St Andrews.

Christopher Holdsworth is Professor of Mediæval History, University of Exeter.

Robert Markus is Emeritus Professor of Mediæval History, University of Nottingham.

John Matthews is Fellow and Tutor in Ancient History, The Queen's College, Oxford.

Roger Ray is Professor of History, University of Toledo, Ohio.

B.H. Warmington is Reader in Ancient History, University of Bristol.

T.P. Wiseman is Professor of Classics, University of Exeter.

MAIN ABBREVIATIONS USED

ACW	*Ancient Christian Writers*, ed. J. Quasten and J.C. Plumpe (Westminster, Maryland/London 1946–)
AJAH	*American Journal of Ancient History*
ASE	*Anglo-Saxon England*, ed. Peter Clemoes (Cambridge 1972–)
BAR	*British Archaeological Reports.*
BEFAR	*Bibliothèque des écoles françaises d'Athènes et de Rome*
BJRL	*Bulletin of the John Rylands Library*
Byz.Zeit	*Byzantinische Zeitschrift*
CC	*Corpus Christianorum*
Chastag-nol,	*Fastes*, A. Chastagnol, *Les Fastes de la préfecture de Rome au Bas-Empire* (Paris 1962)
CJ	*Codex Justinianus*
CLA	E.A. Lowe, *Corpus Latini Antiquiores*
CQ	*Classical Quarterly*
CSEL	*Corpus Scriptorum Latinorum*
CT	*Codex Theodosianus*
DOP	*Dumbarton Oaks Papers*
DTC	*Dictionnaire de Théologie Catholique*, ed. A. Vacant, E. Mangenot, E. Amann, 15 vols. (Paris 1903–50)
EHR	*English Historical Review*
JEH	*Journal of Ecclesiastical History*
JHS	*Journal of Hellenic Studies*
JRS	*Journal of Roman Studies*
MEFR	*Mélanges d'archéologie et d'historie d'Ecole Française de Rome*
MGH	*Monumenta Germaniae Historica inde ab a.c.500 usque ad a. 1500*, ed. G.H. Pertz and others
AA	*Auctores Antiquissimi*
Epp	*Epistolae*
Leges	*Leges in Folio*
SRL	*Scriptores rerum langobardicarum et italicarum*
SRM	*Scriptores rerum merovingicarum*
SS	*Scriptores*
PBSR	*Papers of the British School at Rome*
PL	*Patrologia Latina*, ed. J.P. Migne
PLRE	*Prosopography of the Later Roman Empire*, A.H.M. Jones, J.R. Martindale and J. Morris, vol.1
PW	*Paulys Realencyklopadie der klassichen Altertums-wissenschaft*, new ed. G. Wissowa and W. Kroll
RAC	*Reallexicon für Antike und Christentum* (Stuttgart 1941–)

RB	*Revue Bénédictine*
RE	Realencyclopädié für protestantische Theologie, ed. A Hanck, 2 vols. (3rd ed. Leipzig 1896–1913)
RSR	*Revue des sciences religieuses*
RTAM	*Recherches de théologie ancienne et mediévale*
TAPA	*Transactions of the American Philological Association*
ZKG	*Zeitschrift für Kirchengeschichte*

INTRODUCTION: CLASSICAL HISTORIOGRAPHY

Historia vero testis temporum, lux veritatis, vita memoriae, magistra vitae, nuntia vetustatis...

How did the ancient world believe history should be written? The most succinct answer to that question comes in Cicero's treatise *On the orator.* One could hardly ask for a better authority — the first great master of Latin prose style, the interpreter of Greek literary culture to his fellow-Romans, a man of experience with a sense of the breadth of humane studies that took him beyond the schematic rules and categories of mere pedagogic instruction.

Cicero refers to history in book II of the *de oratore*, where 'Antonius' is maintaining the universal scope of the orator's competence — political and forensic oratory, of course, but also ethical persuasion, praise, blame, consolation and so on:[1]

> As for history, which is time's witness, the light of truth, the survival of memory, the instructor of human life and the reporter of the past, whose voice but the orator's can entrust it to immortality?

'The instructor of human life' — in the context of the orator's ethical function, history takes its place as a means of moral education. Through 'Antonius', Cicero was attacking the rhetorical theorists' crude division of oratory into political, forensic and epideictic ('display'), the last of which consisted mainly of panegyric and its converse (*psogos*, censure). History was regarded as closely related to, and in some people's view even a subdivision of, epideictic oratory;[2] for Cicero, and for the greatest of the Roman historians themselves,[3] what that meant was the historian's duty to praise and blame as he saw fit, to produce examples of moral behaviour for his readers to imitate or avoid.

As 'Antonius' develops his theme, that the rhetoricians' third category should be understood as the whole range of moral exhortation, he comes back naturally to history.[4] After a digression on the state of the art, and the inadequacy of Roman historians vis-à-vis Greek, he sums up the aims and methods of historiography as follows:[5]

> Everyone knows history's first law, not to dare to say anything false, and its second, not to be afraid to say anything true. There must be no suspicion of partiality or malice in what the historian writes. These foundations are of course familiar to everyone; as for the building itself, that rests on the subject matter and the language.

The rule for *subject-matter* demands an ordering of times and a description of places. The reader of important events worthy of record expects first what was planned, then what was done, and finally what resulted. So it demands also, as regards the plans, an indication of what the author approves; in the narrative of events, a statement not only of what was done or said but of how it was done or said; and when it comes to results, an explanation of the causes (chance, wisdom or rashness) and an account of the individuals involved — not just their deeds but the life and character of such as are particularly famous.

As for the rule for *language*, the type of style to be followed is fluent and copious, flowing along with a certain smoothness and placidity, avoiding both the roughness of our court-room style and the stinging epigrams of the Forum.

Not everyone accepted Cicero's stylistic view of how the historian should write, but otherwise this summary account of the genre is a fair representation of what both Greeks and Romans thought historiography ought to be.[6] On the Greek side, the tradition survived without interruption into Byzantine historiography; for the Latin West there is the usual hiatus in our knowledge between the late Empire and the Carolingian revival, but at least the *de oratore* survived for men like Einhard to study in the ninth century.[7] It is reasonable therefore to take this passage as our starting-point for the 'inheritance of historiography', and to pick out a few of the items in Cicero's discussion which had a significant after-life in the early middle ages.

The first point is implicit in the context itself. History has a purpose. True, the historian must give his reader pleasure,[8] but that purely literary aim is not enough. *Delectatio* without *utilitas* is the province of the poet. The usefulness of history might be thought of in practical terms (instruction by example in politics and war), or more generally, as Cicero implies, for the reader's moral guidance.[9] Either way, the historian was asking himself, not just what happened, but what lessons his readers would draw from his account.

That leads to the second point, what Cicero described as the 'foundations' of the edifice of history. To be valid as a lesson, history must be true. A simple rule, but what exactly does it mean? Cicero's formulation, echoed by the historians themselves, shows that what he had in mind was partiality and malice — the abuse, as it were, of the power to praise or blame.[10] Mere tendentiousness, however, is not the only way a historian can subvert the truth. When Cicero says 'don't say anything false', he means 'don't lie'. But does he also mean 'don't invent'?

Inventio was the finding of material. For the orator, it was defined as 'the devising of matter, true or plausible, that would make the case convincing'.[11] Aristotle distinguished proofs that the orator must *find*, by arguments from probability arising out of the case itself, from those 'not furnished by ourselves but already in existence', such as the evidence of witnesses and documents;[12] and it could be naively argued that since the historian's material fell in the latter category, he had no need of *inventio*.[13] But a moment's thought reveals how schematic the distinction is: historians constantly resort to arguments from probability to supplement the evidence their witnesses and documents provide, and we can often see them 'devising matter true or plausible' in exactly the orator's manner.[14] History was close to oratory: those who wrote it and those who read it had been educated in the rhetorical schools, and did naturally what they had been trained to do. Totally free invention would count as 'saying what is false', but *inventio* of appropriate and plausible material consistent with what data there were would surely not fall under Cicero's ban. Like Thucydides' treatment of speeches,[15] it would count as the sort of thing that must have happened, and therefore legitimate as history.

So much for the 'foundations'. When Cicero turns to the rules for subject matter, he puts chronology and geography first. Both 'the ordering of times' and 'the description of places' gave rise to important sub-genres as early as the fifth century B.C.[16] The chronicle form was highly developed by the second century B.C., when Apollodorus produced his great work in Pergamum; extended by Nepos and others to include Roman and other western data, it comfortably accommodated the Christian perspective in the hands of Eusebius and his successors.[17] As for geography, including as it did the origins of peoples, its influence as a branch of historiography extended both to the ethnographical treatise (Tacitus' *Germania*) and to ethnic history like that of Cassiodorus on the Goths.[18]

Cicero's schematic formula of plans, events and results need not detain us, except to note the natural inclusion of speeches as part of the historian's material ('not only what was said but how it was said' offers wide scope for *inventio*),[19] and the necessity, as part of historical explanation, of giving an account of the life and character of prominent individuals. That brings us to the question of biography.

The classic statement is by Plutarch in the preface to his *Alexander*:[20]

> I am writing biography, not history; and often a man's most brilliant actions prove nothing as to his character, while some trifling incident, some casual remark or jest, will throw more light upon what manner of man he was than the bloodiest battle, the greatest array of armies, or the most important siege...It is my duty to dwell especially upon those actions which

reveal the workings of my heroes' minds, and from these to construct the portraits of their respective lives, leaving their battles and their great deeds to be recorded by others.

However, the distinction was not always rigorously observed; nor could it be, when praise, blame and moral judgement were among the purposes of history. Historical encomia, like that of Polybius on Philopoemen, or accounts of a great man's youth and education, like those of Onesicritus on Alexander and Nicolaus of Damascus on Augustus, clearly overlapped to a great extent with the biographer's work;[21] and in any case, a single prominent figure, his deeds and his character, might well be used by a historian to shape his work and provide him with a coherent subject.[22]

Once again we must remember the context of Cicero's passage on history; it is associated with *laudatio* as part of his moral reinterpretation of 'epideictic oratory'.[23] History and panegyric were not the same thing. But they were related, as were history and biography, history and epic poetry, history and tragic drama — and contamination by the conventions of those other genres was both easy and common. What was difficult and rare in the ancient world was historical thinking in the modern sense.

The classical tradition of historiography was not a simple phenomenon. There was a great range of both theory and practice for its post-classical inheritors to follow, whether in the continuous tradition of the Greek world or the more haphazardly influenced culture of the Latin West.[24] For what sort of audience was the later historian writing? How far was he constrained by his chosen genre? How pressing were the demands of his contemporary context, for instance in the incorporation of a Christian perspective?

It was to explore such questions that the colloquium on 'Historiography Ancient and Medieval' was held in Exeter in January 1985. The selection of papers which follows concentrates on the half-millennium from the fourth century to the ninth, from the threatened empire of Athanasius and Ammianus to the little worlds of Agnellus and Asser. Despite the great range of time, space and subject-matter, all the nine authors discussed below owed something, great or small, to the complex of precepts and prejudices Cicero and his readers had taken for granted in a different world.

NOTES

1. Cic. *de or.* II 35f.
2. Cic. *orator* 37–42, 65f, 207 (esp. 37 'laudationum et historiarum et talium suasionum', 65 'huic generi historia finitima est'); also Cic. *part. orat.* 70f on *epideixis* and *narratio*. See *Rhet. Graec.* (ed. Spengel) I 399, II 417 etc; also II 70 on rhetorical exercises as essential in the education of historians as well as orators.
3. See for instance Cic. *fam.* V 12.4, Livy *pref.* 10, Tac. *Ann.* III 65, IV 33.
4. Cic. *de or.* II 51–64 (the context is Catulus' objection about *laudationes*, 43–65); see especially §§50 and 64 on *cohortatio*.
5. *de or.* II 62–4, introduced at 62 with 'videtisne quantum munus sit *oratoris* historia?'.
6. For Greek opinion, see Lucian's treatise *How to write history* (translated by K. Kilburn in vol. VI of the Loeb edition), with the commentary of G. Avenarius, *Lukians Schrift zu Geschichtsschreibung* (Meisenheim am Glan 1956).
7. For the textual history, see M. Winterbottom, R.H. Rouse and M.D. Reeve in *Texts and Transmission* (ed. L.D. Reynolds, Oxford 1983) 103f.
8. On *delectatio*, see Tony Woodman in *Creative Imitation and Latin Literature* (ed. D. West and T. Woodman, Cambridge 1979) 154f and 235.
9. See P. Scheller, *De hellenistica historiae conscribendae arte* (Leipzig 1911) 72–8 on different types of usefulness.
10. Sall. *Cat.* 4.2, *Hist.* I 6M, Livy *pref.* 5, Tac. *Hist.* I 1, *Ann.* I 1, etc; F.R.D. Goodyear, *The Annals of Tacitus* I (Cambridge 1972) 100f. Lucian's criterion of truth in history was the same: *How to write history* 40f, 61. See now N.F. Partner in *Classical Rhetoric and Medieval Historiography* (ed. E. Breisach, Kalamazoo 1985) 11.
11. *Rhetorica ad Herennium* I 3, trans. H. Caplan (Loeb ed.); Cic. *de inv.* I 9.
12. Ar. *Rhet.* I 2.2, 15.1–2: the 'unartificial' proofs are defined as laws, witnesses, contracts, torture, oaths.
13. Thus Lucian, *How to write history* 50, explicitly in contrast with oratory: 'What historians have to relate is fact and will speak for itself, for it has already happened: what is required is arrangement and exposition. So they must look not for what to say but how to say it.' He goes on to compare historians with sculptors, whose 'material was before them' — using the same word Aristotle used for his 'unartificial proofs'. See p.71f below.
14. I cite a trivial but explicit example, Plutarch's idea (based on a derivation of *Talasio* from the Greek *talasia*) that the Sabine women were reconciled with their captors by an agreement that nothing more than spinning should be asked of them: Plut. *Rom.* 15.3 ('a more credible reason might be conjectured as follows'), 19.7 (assumed as fact in the narrative).
15. Thuc. I 22.1: 'my aim has been to reproduce what seemed to me the most probable and appropriate language for each occasion'.
16. See C.W. Fornara, *The Nature of History in Ancient Greece and Rome* (Berkeley and Los Angeles 1983) 12–16, 28f; Fornara's exclusion of them from 'history' proper is, as he half admits (p.3), quite inconsistent with the usage of the Greeks and Romans themselves.
17. F. Jacoby, *Fragmente der griechischen Historiker* IIB (Leiden 1962) 992–1229, nos. 239–61; Brian Croke in *History and Historians in Late Antiquity* (ed. B. Croke and A.M. Emmett, Sydney 1983) 116–31.
18. Cf. Professor Bullough's paper below. Origins of peoples: e.g. Sall. *Jug.* 17–19, *Hist.* III 61–80M (*situs Africae* and *situs Ponti* respectively); cf. Catullus 9.7 ('loca facta nationes'), Tac. *Ann.* IV 33 ('situs *gentium*').
19. Cf. p.80f below (Bede on the Synod of Whitby).
20. Plut. *Alex.* 1.2–3, trans. Stewart and Long (1889).

21. Diog. Laert. VI 84 (Onesicritus), Suda *s.v. Nikolaos Damaskenos*, Pol. X 21.5–8; A. Momigliano, *The Development of Greek Biography* (Harvard 1971) 82–4, cf. Fornara, *op.cit.* (n.16) 34–6, 185–8.
22. As Cicero suggested to Lucceius at *fam.* V 12.2: 'si uno in argumento unaque in persona mens tua tota versabitur ...'.
23. Cic. *de or.* II 43–6 and 65 on *laudationes*; cf. n.4 above.
24. See Croke and Emmett, *op.cit.* (n.17) 1–12.

I

DID ATHANASIUS WRITE HISTORY?

B.H. Warmington

The most convenient edition of most of the works here considered is that by William Bright (Oxford 1881) with an introduction still useful. The title Bright gave to his edition was 'St Athanasius' Historical Writings', and he includes the following: *Epistula Encyclica* (dated to 340); *Apologia contra Arianos* (350, with a brief addition in our recensions in 358); *Epistula ad Episcopos Aegypti et Libyae* (early 356) — strictly a theological work; *Apologia ad Constantium* (356); *Apologia de Fuga* (357/8); *Epistula ad Serapionem de Morte Arii* (358 or 340)[1], *Historia Arianorum* (358), normally associated, as by Bright, with an *Epistula ad Monachos* (358 or 340); and *Epistula de Synodis* (359). Robertson's edition of the translations of works by Athanasius, also with a most useful introduction, in the Library of Nicene and Post-Nicene Fathers (Oxford 1892) added three further letters and the *Vita Antonii* to what he described as 'historical or historico-polemical works'. This paper considers only those listed in Bright's edition because the letters added by Robertson are brief and unimportant, and because the problems raised by the *Vita Antonii* are too complex for the space available.[2] One additional work is considered on its own merits; it is a circular letter issued by the Egyptian bishops, and bearing all the marks of Athanasian authorship, written in 339 and included among the documents reproduced in the later *Apologia contra Arianos*.

The works are described as historical because they give accounts, of varied lengths and complexity, both of individual incidents and of complex developments in church politics from *c.* 320 to 360, in which Athanasius' own life and actions were inextricably mixed. But it is obvious that in form at any rate none save the *Historia Arianorum* corresponds to historical writing as understood in antiquity; they are either epistolary or apologetic. Yet in the epistolary category we are not talking, save in the letter to Serapio, of private letters written to a personal friend, or even of letters carefully written with a view to later, posthumous publication, but of letters which would have a wide and immediate circulation. General letters would certainly go out in some hundreds of copies to ecclesiastics over a large portion of the Empire. The impression of immediacy is strengthened by the clustering of the dates of composition in the years immediately following his second and third exiles. The only exception is the *Apologia contra Arianos* of 350, but for that too an immediate need can perhaps be detected.

Athanasius himself rarely uses the word *historia* in one of its main meanings, a piece of historical narrative, but it occurs three times in the *Epistula Encyclica* of his account of a specific event — his replacement at Alexandria by Gregory in 339 — and also of the story in the Old Testament which he uses as an analogy. The high point of this document is a highly coloured and pathetic account of the scenes of intimidation, violence and looting which, he says, accompanied the physical take-over of his church. The effect which he wanted to produce is signalled by a rhetorical question: have such deeds as this ever been made the subject of tragedy among the ancients, or has the like ever happened before in time of persecution or war? It need hardly be said that even Athanasius' description of the event hardly matches what we might expect from such exaggerated language, which has a similarity with that in the letter of the Egyptian bishops of the preceding year, describing violence said to have been perpetrated by the Mareotis Commission, and with that narrating the second occasion on which Athanasius was removed, and his church occupied by force, this time in 356.[3] No doubt the violence took place, but it has been written up in rhetorical style, just as analogous scenes of the storming of cities were written up in Greek and Roman historiography.[4] The point is however that we are at best reading 'instant history', written to publicise an event as widely as possible. The world of Athanasius and the church communicated like the world of the late Roman imperial bureaucracy, in which, as is well known, there was a prolific increase in the production of letters and documents of all sorts resulting from the growth of the administration under the Tetrarchy and second Flavians. We can see this happening in reverse in the *de Synodis* in which, while living in retreat in rural Egypt, Athanasius was able to give a preliminary account of what had happened at the councils of Ariminum in Italy and Isaurian Seleucia within weeks of their meetings.

About a decade later, *c.* 350, Athanasius wrote the best known and most highly praised work in the collection, the *Apologia contra Arianos*. It is probable that this too was called for by specific circumstances. Athanasius had been permitted by Constantius to return to Alexandria as bishop in 346, his replacement Gregory having died in 345. It seems that attacks on him, repeating the grounds for his condemnation at Tyre in 335, were being renewed in spite of, or more probably because of, his return, to such a degree that Athanasius wanted to publicise not merely his vindication, as he viewed it, by three later councils but also a detailed defence against all that had been alleged against him since 328 and for which he had been condemned at Tyre. It has been the usual view that the death of Constans in January 350 gave Athanasius cause for concern about his position, or revived the hopes of his opponents in the East; while not impossible, this depends on how much weight is put on the hypothesis of the influence of Constans in procuring his return.[5] The majority of eastern bishops will have seen no reason to view his condemnation at Tyre as having been overturned by a council of Egyptian bishops, inevitably subservient to Alexandria, or western councils at Rome and Serdica.

The feature of the *Apologia contra Arianos* which has attracted most favourable attention is its incorporation of no less than 36 verbatim texts of documents, including a dozen from the hands of emperors. This compares with, for example, the 15 imperial documents in Eusebius' *Life of Constantine*. The purposes of the two authors were however quite different, even though we may suppose Eusebius' great contribution to historical science, the incorporation of *Urkunden*, was the model. Eusebius wished his documents to illustrate aspects of his hero's pious life: Athanasius incorporated his for strictly legal purposes; they are proofs, like the testimony of witnesses or the recitation of laws in the law-courts. He expressly says that the defence as such is addressed to the sincere, the proofs to the contentious.

The documents illustrating the years from 325 to 335 in effect support the earlier letter of the Egyptian bishops of 339/340, the narrative of which is adapted for the *Apologia*. The work presents Athanasius as the victim of a host of enemies comprehensively and vaguely labelled 'Eusebius and his associates' or just 'Arians' and should be viewed in the light of ancient advocacy, even though it was for distribution rather than for delivery in a court of law. Naturally Athanasius' version of events has not gone undisputed, but attention has tended to concentrate on specific points, for example, his treatment of the Meletian case, where exceptionally we happen to have some independent evidence.[6] But if we have regard for its form and purpose, we cannot deduce from it much that is certain even about the specific charges made against him, still less about the evidence produced by his opponents, because like any advocate he concentrated not on the strongest but on the weakest part of his opponents' case, such as his alleged murder of Arsenius. Again, the apparently detailed rebuttal of the charge of sacrilege is a piece of forensic obfuscation which leaves little doubt that there was in fact a discreditable incident of some sort. Nor should we forget the obvious point that he has only included those documents which he believed supported his case. A century later, Sozomen, in his introductory remarks[7] on the sources available for his Ecclesiastical History — remarks which are superior to most analogous passages in classical historians — made a general criticism, without giving names, of such one-sided collections of documents assembled, as he says, by polemicists of differing groups. Although Sozomen was orthodox and wrote favourably of Athanasius elsewhere, the *Apologia contra Arianos* was precisely such a collection as he condemned.

In February 356 the *dux Aegypti* Syrianus with an armed force seized the church named Theonas at Alexandria. Athanasius escaped, or was allowed to leave, and spent the next six years if not actually on the run at least in more or less private and obscure retreats in parts of Egypt. The years eventually saw a stream of writings — the theological *Epistula ad episcopos Aegypti et Libyae* and the *Apologia ad Constantium*, both of 356, the *Apologia de fuga* of 358, an addition to the *Apologia contra Arianos* which presupposes a fresh 'edition', and finally the *Historia Arianorum*. The purpose of all these was to inform his followers of events and to retain their loyalty in the face of pressure from the organs of state, and the presence of an opposing element in the Egyptian church, as well as Christians indifferent to the dispute, whose strength is rarely glimpsed in his accounts.[8]

The *Apologia de fuga* is in part like the *Epistula encyclica* of 339, a piece of 'instant history' giving an account of the seizure of his church at Alexandria, and in part a defence of his flight. But the *Apologia ad Constantium* is very different, and in spite of its conventional title is not an apologia like that of 350, about to be reissued. It contains more references to secular history than any other of his works. Athanasius adopted the formal style suitable for an address to the Augustus, and the courtly language objected to by stern critics in the last century.[9] He was concerned to rebut four allegations, all of which could be interpreted as treason, which he says were being made by his enemies: that he had tried (before 350) to set the emperor Constans against his brother, that he had subsequently corresponded with the usurper Magnentius, that he had used the church built at the emperor's expense at Alexandria before it had been completed and its use authorised by the emperor, and that he had disobeyed an imperial order to come to Italy. The text is quite clear that the defence was not delivered before the emperor, and the probability is that the form was adopted because of the political nature of the allegations Athanasius felt he had to counter.

It is certain that none of the charges led to a formal trial, and it is legitimate to doubt whether the other quasi-treasonable charges which Athanasius elsewhere says had been levelled against him earlier, under Constantine, were taken seriously.[10] We only have his bare assertion for any of them, later references being derivative. This is not to say that such allegations were not made during his stormy career, but evidence that they, rather than theological or ecclesiastical issues, were the 'real' grounds for his exiles is hard to come by. After all, Constantine, when irritated for religious reasons with Eusebius of Nicomedia in 325, suddenly announced[11] that the bishop had been an active spy for Licinius, and that he could prove it, but no trial took place and Eusebius was back in good standing within three years. Emperors, we may suppose, could normally distinguish between potentially serious cases of treason and make-weight attacks made in controversies about other matters. Neither Athanasius, Eusebius of Nicomedia, Eustathius of Antioch[12] nor, as far as we know, any other bishop against whom such allegations were made, suffered the horrendous consequences of a trial for treason as described so frequently for the same period of time by Ammianus Marcellinus. If Athanasius had really feared that sort of thing, the *Apologia ad Constantium* would not have been so cool or literary a production.

The work which at first sight is most similar to traditional historical writing is the so-called *Historia Arianorum* (no evidence of the original title exists). There are substantial difficulties in the traditional view that it is associated with the letter *ad monachos*.[13] Furthermore, Robertson argued against Bright that we have a complete work, not one of which the first half is lost, in spite of the abrupt beginning. He makes the analogy of Xenophon's *Hellenica*, the opening words of which follow straight on from the conclusion of Thucydides; so the *Historia Arianorum* follows directly the conclusion of the *Apologia contra Arianos* in its original form.

The contrast with the two apologies is marked, especially in that it contains a ferocious attack on Constantius, who is compared unfavourably with Saul, Ahab, Belshazzar, Pontius Pilate and others. The same writers who have deplored the courtly language of the *Apologia ad Constantium* have deplored the vulgar abuse contained in the *Historia Arianorum*. But it is not necessary to assume some change in circumstances to explain the difference in tone. Athanasius had already used the forms of a legalistic defence based on documents, and a dignified apologia against allegations of high political crimes. In the *Historia Arianorum* he turns to the attack with many of the techniques of ancient polemic. The history of his vicissitudes since 335, treated legalistically in the *Apologia contra Arianos*, is here narrated with the emphasis on his enemies' manipulation of the emperor. In contrast with the other works, in which Athanasius writes in the first person, he now uses the third. One can only guess at the reason for his use of this technique, known to us most obviously in the case of Caesar's *commentarii*. One of the notable and more regrettable similarities with traditional historiography is that instead of original documents we have speeches or other material in *oratio recta* which are in fact the compositions of the author. Most are said to be private conversations between the emperor and Arian bishops.

It is not worth asking where Athanasius could have got his information from: the device is transparent, and in the *de Synodis* Athanasius himself reveals it. After describing in *oratio recta* alleged schemes of Arian bishops he says 'even if they did not speak these words, everything they did was with these intentions'.[14] It is desirable to make the point, stressed already by Bright, because even today passages out of such compositions have been used as if they were statements of fact by Athanasius.[15]

The *Historia Arianorum* has always been considered of doubtful reliability, and errors of fact in the other works have been noted. But there are more general points to be made when considering these works of Athanasius. In general, the church and the Christian religion itself occupy a very small place in the pages of Ammianus Marcellinus, and Athanasius himself gets barely a mention.[16] On the other hand the Persian wars, the campaign against Magnentius, and the Gallus affair, together with the other secular concerns of Ammianus, had just as small a place in the pages of Athanasius. We are looking as it were at two circles with only the smallest of intersections. It is of course well known that in the fourth century and later the secular or 'classicising' historians had little or nothing to say about Christianity. The converse is less often remarked — the almost complete lack of concern that Christian writers, at least those who were ecclesiastics, had for secular affairs.

The Athanasian view is in fact characterised more often that not by a marked hostility to the state, or at any rate to the apparatus of the state. This is expressed with varying intensity and is most marked in the *Historia Arianorum*, but it occurs as early as the letter of the Egyptian bishops of 339.[17] Modern studies of the relations between the state and the church in the fourth century have frequently remarked that attacks on the actions of the state, whether from Donatist, Arian or Catholic sources, were only made when the faction concerned had felt their force, and that each was willing to ask for the support of the emperor. This is no doubt just, but another way of looking at it is that all Christians, or at any rate the vocal ecclesiastics, shared a view of the church as an entity essentially separate from the state — a 'new people' in fact. The veneration of martyrs kept the memory of persecution alive and thus any faction could make polemical points by associating its opponents with the organs of the state. It is not surprising that the eastern bishops at Serdica protested[18] about support given by *comites* and *duces* to Athanasius, when he returned from Gaul in 337, in terms similar to those used by Athanasius himself about support given by these and other administrators — prefects of Egypt, imperial *notarii* and *palatini*[19] — to his opponents. His descriptions of the violence used by soldiers during the seizure of the churches at Alexandria[20] are similar to, and more effective than, those in Donatist sources, more frequently referred to in modern times.

It is perhaps a paradox to find that in the history of his world, the world of the church and his own part in its affairs, Athanasius finds little cause to bring in the supernatural — less indeed than many a classical historian. Councils which condemned him are no more seriously condemned as instruments of the devil than those which supported him are inspired by God. Occasions on which divine judgment is seen are few and trivial, and Athanasius is relatively restrained even in his account of the death of Arius in a public convenience at Constantinople.[21] The actions of individuals are determined by their virtues, or more frequently their vices (envy, malice, wrong-thinking), analogous to, though not the same as, those which so concerned the secular historians; the nature of the theological issues which divided them receives hardly a mention.

Athanasius faced a problem common to all writers, and not just historians, of Roman imperial date — how to describe and explain imperial decision making. At all times it was necessary to rely on what was little better than gossip about what went on at meetings of the emperor's *consilium* or *consistorium*, and on what other influences at court might be at work. This needs no more illustration than, say, the alleged roles of the imperial freedmen under Claudius, the courtiers of Commodus, and the eunuchs of Constantius. In fact, the role of the eunuchs is the only major point of contact between Athanasius and Ammianus;[22] having spent some time in showing the Arians personally interviewing the emperor, he states that they really achieved their purpose through the support of the eunuchs, in particular Eusebius *praepositus sacri cubiculi*. But his normal view is that Constantius reached decisions in religious matters through intrigues by bishops who had access to him — men like Eusebius of Nicomedia, Valens of Mursa and Ursacius of Singidunum. Intriguing bishops thus have the same role, as agents in a general conspiracy theory, as emperors' wives, freedmen, eunuchs or secretaries[23] do in other writers. This, at least, is when the imperial decision is unfavourable to Athanasius. But when an emperor decides in his favour, as Contantine did on several occasions before 335, in spite of the alleged intrigues of 'Eusebius and his associates', the decision is his own,[24] no question of the advice of friends or supporters of Athanasius at court.

The ultimate victory of Athanasius was never a foregone conclusion. His so-called historical works, largely grouped[25] in periods when his position was seriously weakened by his expulsion from his see, the source of his power, were all polemical works and testify to a need to present his case immediately and forcefully to as wide a readership as possible. They were addressed in the first instance to his supporters in Egypt, where he was not without opposition through most of his career. He also needed to win support in the west. The readership appears to have been exclusively ecclesiastic (including some of the monastic communities in Egypt), though it is possible that an educated lay readership could have been reached by the *Apologia ad Constantium*. The clerical view predominates even in small things; when Athanasius wished to find analogies for the 'tyranny' of Constantius, he chose Biblical villains rather than the standard tyrants from a rhetorician's handbook. This viewpoint is narrower than that of Eusebius, for all that the latter more than anyone had demonstrated that the church as a 'new people' had its own history as well as a theology and philosophy; Eusebius, in the *Life of Constantine*, had formally compared his hero with Cyrus and Alexander, besides justifying the utility of his work compared with those written on Nero and even more deplorable persons.[26]

The variety of Athanasius' apologetic styles is impressive — epistolary, legalistic, courtly and abusive. His canons of relevance are strict, and nothing is allowed to divert the reader from the essential, the fortunes of Athanasius himself. No other person, not even Constantius, appears as a real individual in the *corpus*. His enemies are blanketed without discrimination in all-purpose phrases — 'associates of Eusebius' in events up to *c.* 341, and 'Arians' even more frequently for subsequent years.[27] A few names are given and we can glimpse a hard core of inveterate opponents, but their real theological positions are merely abused, and their aims and purposes described with the same partisanship as those of the enemies of Cicero and Demosthenes. Athanasius, in short, was as much a master of the techniques of forensic as of deliberative rhetoric.[28]

The *Historia Arianorum* could, very crudely, perhaps be regarded as analogous to *commentarii* in the Roman sense and hence as material for future historians. Certainly it was one of the works of Athanasius which provided such material for a later generation. When Socrates Scholasticus in the 430s decided to write a continuation of Eusebius' *Ecclesiastical History* he started by following Rufinus, but rewrote the early part of his work when he came across the works of Athanasius.[29] This was an improvement, but it must reinforce the almost total dependence on Athanasius' works of all subsequent efforts to understand the church politics of this era. The amount of good information from other sources is negligible.[30] In the last decade or so serious attempts have been made to reassess, or perhaps to rescue, the theology of Arius, almost submerged by Athanasius and later polemic.[31] An attempt to review the actual course of events and the nature of the struggle within the church from 325 to 362 would have to start from a full appreciation of the uniformly apologetic nature of the so-called historical works of Athanasius. Who, after all, could write with confidence an account of the relations between Philip of Macedon and Athens on the sole basis of the speeches of Demosthenes? To use another analogy, the amount of serious criticism devoted to the Athanasian version of the relations between Constantius and the church is a minute proportion of that devoted to the Tacitean picture of Tiberius and his relations with the Senate.

NOTES

1. For the alternative dates of this work and of the *ad Monachos*, see n. 13.
2. *RAC* I, 863 ff. summarises recent views on the *Vita Antonii*.
3. *Apol. c. Arianos* 15 (Mareotis Commission); *Hist. Ar.* 55, cp. *de Fuga* 6, 7.
4. Quintilian 8, 3, 68 summarises the requirements and regards such scenes as obligatory for historical writing.
5. The story that the return was due to the threats of Constans, which occurs in the late church historians, stems from the deplorable Rufinus, and should be rejected. It perhaps derived from Rufinus' interpretation of *Apol. ad Constantium* 2 ff. Gwatkin, who criticised many of the fables in Rufinus, accepted this one, *Studies in Arianism* (Cambridge 1883), 126.
6. H.I. Bell, *Jews and Christians in Egypt* (London 1914), 38ff.
7. Sozomen I, 1.
8. See e.g. the second letter *ad Monachos* and the guarded remark in *ad Serap.* 5.
9. e.g. Bright, *ed. cit.* 1xiii ff. and Robertson *ed. cit.* 267.
10. *Apol. c. Arianos* (imposing a 'linen tax' on Egypt; being hostile to the emperor and bribing Philumenos); 87 (threatening to hold back corn supplies from Alexandria to Constantinople). He never seems to have felt it necessary to rebut these charges.
11. Opitz, *Urkunden* 27 (Constantine's letter to the Nicomedian church, late 325).
12. Athanasius implies that the real cause of the deposition and exile of Eustathius was that he had insulted the emperor's mother, *Apol. c. Arianos*, 4.
13. C. Kannengiesser, *Athanase d'Alexandrie, évêque et écrivain: une lecture des traités contre les Ariens* (Paris, 1983), 374 ff. puts substantial arguments in favour of dating the *ad Monachos* and the *ad Serapionem* to *c.* 340 rather than *c.* 358. The traditional association of the *ad Monachos* with the *Hist. Ar.* had already been doubted by Robertson, *ed. cit.* 267 ff.
14. *de Synodis* 7; see Bright, *ed. cit.* 1xxvii.
15. T.D. Barnes, 'Emperors and Bishops in the Fourth Century A.D.: Some Problems', *AJAH* 3 (1978) 56 ff. uses *Hist. Ar.* 42 to support the thesis that Ossius of Cordova presided at Nicea; repeated in *Constantine and Eusebius* (Harvard 1981), 215.
16. Amm. Marc. XV, 7, 7 and 10, interesting as a pagan view of the reasons for his deposition.
17. *Apol. c. Arianos* 8, the council of Tyre invalid because it was 'presided over' by an imperial *comes* and his officials.
18. *CSEL* LXV, 53.
19. e.g. *Hist. Ar.* 10, 15, 29, 37.
20. *Ep. Encyc.* 3, 4; *de Fuga* 6, 7.
21. *ad Serapionem de Morte Arii.*
22. Athanasius *Hist. Ar.* 35 ff. Amm. Marc, XIV, 11, XVIII, 4, 2 ff.
23. Athanasius' younger contemporary, the sophist Libanius, objected strongly to the influence of *notarii* in the time of Constantius.
24. *Apol. c. Arianos* 60 ff.

25. The revised dates proposed by Kannengiesser (above, n. 13) make no difference to the argument.
26. *VC* I, 7; 10 (Nero). Admittedly Eusebius also compared Constantine to Moses.
27. It would be otiose to count the number of occasions on which Athanasius uses the expression οἱ περὶ Εὐσέβιον.
28. G.C. Stead, 'Rhetorical Method in Athanasius', *Vigiliae Christianae* 30 (1976) 120 ff, demonstrates his use of the latter in his theological works.
29. Socrates II, 1. The dubious authority of Rufinus (on which see briefly Gwatkin *op cit.* 93 ff.) is not improved by demonstrating his dependence on the shadowy Gelasius of Caesarea.
30. It should be repeated that Socrates, Sozomen and Theodoret can only occasionally be quoted as independent sources for the early and middle fourth century. A century ago Gwatkin (*op. cit.* 98) properly referred to 'the spurious authority of a long line of copyists'.
31. e.g. R. Gregg and D. Groh, *Early Arianism : a View of Salvation* (London and Philadelphia 1981), with further references.

II

AMMIANUS AND THE ETERNITY OF ROME

John Matthews

I

It is a constantly intriguing paradox that the last great Latin historian of Rome was by birth a Greek from Syrian Antioch, and the last great Latin poet a Greek from Egyptian Alexandria. In the case of Ammianus Marcellinus, the meaning of the paradox is clearer to us in its general than in its particular aspects, for the exact circumstances in which it came about are not know to us — neither when Ammianus went to Rome to complete his history (except that he was there during the later 380s), nor precisely why he went there, nor by what route he travelled. What we do know, from cross-references within the history itself, is that he was still composing, able at least to make some quite substantial insertions, as late as 390, but apparently not (on the evidence) later than this;[1] and, from a letter of Libanius written to him late in 392 but referring to a slightly earlier time, that he gave recitations from his history at Rome to an audience, some of whose members took news of them back to Libanius at Antioch.[2]

This letter of Libanius, praising his compatriot, is the only external reference we possess to Ammianus, the rest of whose life and attitudes must be inferred solely from his own text: and this is itself incomplete. Of 31 original books, running from the principate of Nerva to the battle of Hadrianople in August 378 and its immediate aftermath, the first thirteen books are lost, together of course with the preface in which he may have explained his overall design and purpose.[3] The surviving books (14–31) cover in considerable but sometimes uneven detail, and with an occasionally capricious emphasis on the historian's own experiences, the 25 years 353–378. Despite, or rather as part of, their capriciousness, these books are among the most revealing of late Roman sources. There is no important issue on which they do not have something to say, and I cannot think of any other ancient writer who surpasses Ammianus' powers of observation and his ability through this to convey a visual image and penetrate character — even if, as Arnaldo Momigliano remarked, he is much less adept at defining a situation.[4] He is a fascinating and disconcerting guide to the society he knew; but he still has not told us why he came to Rome.

We are however entitled to draw natural inferences from what we know of Ammianus' background and the cultural milieu in which he grew up. If I may assert briefly what perhaps does not require exhaustive proof, I believe that the Latin language was much more integral to the formation of this Greek than one might at first imagine.[5] Antioch was in the fourth century a frequent imperial residence, and at all times an important centre of administration, military and civil. It would undoubtedly have been affected, and more so than other cities, by the extended franchise of the Latin language in the fourth-century east, a legacy of the much enlarged and vastly more assertive governmental establishment of the Tetrarchs and their successors, in which Latin was the language in normal administrative use, with all the consequences that this implies for its wider diffusion; think for example of the appointment of the African Latinist Lactantius as professor of rhetoric at Nicomedia, the court capital of Diocletian. If I and others are right in attributing Ammianus' early promotion to the rank of *protector domesticus* to paternal influence — a family friendship, perhaps, with the general Ursicinus on whose staff Ammianus served from about 350 for ten years — then the Latin language will have impinged early on Ammianus' upbringing. I suspect, in fact, that he knew it from childhood, as a member of a family connected with the imperial army or administration. Further, Ammianus travelled widely in active service, to Roman Mesopotamia, north Italy, Gaul, the Danubian lands, the Tigris frontier, and under Julian to the Persian capital of Ctesiphon, from where he escaped to Roman territory after the death of Julian, in the embattled retreat that he described with such vivid authenticity: then, after his retirement from active service, to Egypt, Thrace, the Pontic region, and southern Greece, the last while 'passing through' on the way to somewhere else. Where he was going when he 'passed through' Mothone he does not say, nor does he locate the journey in time, except to mention that he saw there the hull of a ship cast inland by the tidal wave that followed the great earthquake of 365. The vessel was now 'gaping apart' from long decay, 'diuturna carie fatiscentem' (26.10.19).

With other readers of Ammianus, I think (and believe it to be formally demonstrable) of Julian the Apostate as the historical inspiration behind Ammianus, linking things he had seen and experienced himself with the broader course of Roman history; while Julian himself by his policies challenged comparison with his Constantinian predecessors and with his second-century model, Marcus Aurelius.[6] Yet Julian the Hellenist, on one occasion called an 'untrustworthy Asian Greek' by resentful Gallic troops (17.9.3) and described by Ammianus, rather smugly perhaps, as possessing an 'adequate' command of Latin (16.5.7), is far from explaining Ammianus' choice of Latin as the language of history. He could perfectly well have chosen Greek, and produced a sort of latter-day Thucydides (better, Polybius), a combination of military history, social diagnosis and delineation of character that would be remarkable in any language. I have seen it suggested, with a nice touch of humour, that Ammianus chose Latin in order to avoid being upstaged by the appearance, in Greek, of the history of his younger contemporary Eunapius. I think, indeed, that Eunapius' history had appeared (in its first edition) by the time that Ammianus wrote, and that Ammianus used him for certain episodes of the Persian campaign which, despite his presence on the campaign, he had not been able to witness himself.[7] It is possible, too, that because of the manner in which his text has been preserved, the qualities of Eunapius have been underestimated by modern critics; but not to such an extent as would justify Ammianus' being deterred by the appearance of his work into an entire change of language. Not all Eunapius' shortcomings can be assigned to his later epitomators, and they must clearly have been visible at the time. One has only to read a few pages of Ammianus to see that his absorption into Roman, and Latin, ideals and ways of thought is in every way too profound to be explained as a late evasive tactic in face of a work of greatly inferior quality to his own.

By the same token, Ammianus' choice cannot simply be explained by his late discovery of the pitiful Latin historical tradition of the fourth century, nor, even, by an encounter with Tacitus. It seems to me quite likely that acquaintance with Tacitus has something to do with Ammianus' extension back from his own into the second and third centuries, and particularly, of course, with the starting-point of the principate of Nerva; but not with the essential character of the history as a deeply engaged account, in Latin, of the contemporary age. Whatever the available models, Ammianus had a choice; he chose Latin, and a Roman idiom, and had surely done so before considering the more detailed tactical dispositions — such as where precisely to start — that a historian will necessarily make in the light of the literary models that seem appropriate to him. I would regard the choice of Rome as the place in which Ammianus would complete the history as a special case of the question why he chose Latin; it stems from and was implicit in an early phase in his development. It follows that Ammianus' attitude to Rome may be expected to throw light on the deeper nature of the paradox with which I began, that of the Greek writing in Latin, and it is with this, leading to related and broader historiographical questions, that I will begin.

II

Urbs aeterna, 'the eternal city', is Ammianus' normal expression for Rome.[8] It is how it appears in the first reference in the surviving text, the prefecture of Rome of Memmius Vitrasius Orfitus in 353–6, and it is this prefecture which brings in the digression (14.6) where Ammianus sets out most fully his ideal of Rome. The city, he here writes, 'will live [or 'conquer', the word *victura* preserving this nice ambiguity] as long as there are men', a happy state of affairs which is the consequence of an 'eternal pact' struck between those old enemies, Virtue and Fortune. Lacking either one or the other, the city would not have reached her summit of greatness.

Ammianus turns now to the growth of Rome, from wars waged around her walls to the dominion of empire, a process compared with the growth of a man from childhood to old age: and to the splendour of the political assemblies, of people and senate, through which, though they were now politically inactive, the greatness of Rome had been forged and in which it was now symbolised. But the splendour of the assemblies is ruined by the conduct of a few individuals ('levitate paucorum incondita') who 'do not reflect where they were born' and yield themselves to licence and ease; *levitas* reads here almost as the formal opposite of Roman *gravitas*. Ammianus now launches into an attack on the conduct of senate and people, of a satirically exuberant character that makes rather surprising his dismissive remark, in another passage, about Juvenal and Marius Maximus as favoured reading-matter of members of the aristocracy (28.4.14). He had introduced his first digression in order to show why it was that whenever his narrative turned to Rome, nothing was to be written of except 'rioting, drunkenness and scandals like these'. Ammianus thinks, or affects to think, that 'foreigners' (*peregrini*) would be particularly surprised by this shocking situation — as perhaps he had been himself, when as a *peregrinus* he first came to Rome.

It is in this connection with urban disorder in its various forms that Ammianus generally presents, at regular intervals, the tenures of office of prefects of Rome.[9] The administrations are characterised by rioting for a variety of reasons, especially corn and wine shortages. On one occasion the cause of rioting is the arrest of a popular charioteer, on another, to which I shall return, the bloody strife surrounding the succession to the bishopric of Rome, waged in one of the major churches of the city.

Another aspect of the eternity of Rome resides in the ancient grandeur of its public buildings. Ammianus conveys this in a famous passage, the triumphal entry to Rome of Constantius in 357 (16.10.1–17). There is no need to transcribe from Ammianus the details he provides of the ceremonial *adventus*, a text-book reference for all similar ceremonies.[10]

Instead, I would draw attention to one particular facet of Ammianus' account, the transition he makes between the entry itself, which is criticised for its inappropriately 'triumphal' character — 'as if the emperor were off to terrify Euphrates or Rhine by a display of arms' — and the emperor's conduct once within the city, 'the home of empire and all the virtues' (16.10.13). Constantius addressed senate and people in the manner appropriate for each, above all he admired the buildings of Rome, his amazement conveyed by Ammianus in a sequence of figures of mounting hyperbole; 'the shrines of Tarpeian Jupiter, excelling as divine things excel human; baths built up like provinces; the Flavian Amphitheatre, to whose summit the human eye can barely reach [we almost hear at this point the cricking of Constantius' neck as he strains upwards, that neck he had held firm, as if in a vice, in order to hold it steady and *prevent* the betrayal of amazement, on his first entry to Rome]; the Pantheon, like an entire rounded city district...'. These were chief among the glories of the eternal city: 'aliaque inter haec decora urbis aeternae' (16.10.14).

Apart from its evocation of Constantius' amazement, the purpose of Ammianus' rhetoric is to convey in physical, architectural terms the theme of the city as mistress of the world, in an application of the '*urbs – orbis*' paradox found in writers down to Jerome and Rutilius Namatianus. A city enshrines the world; so, Rome contains, physically, entire cities; it is a theme picked up by a later visitor to Rome, Olympiodorus of Thebes; 'each of the great houses... contained within itself everything that a medium-sized city could hold — a hippodrome, fora, temples, fountains and baths. To put it briefly [Olympiodorus here breaks into verse]: "One house is a town, the city holds a thousand towns!" '[11]

As for the monuments of Rome as symbols of its eternity, this theme arises also in Ammianus' digression on Alexandria, where among many marvels the Serapeum (Ammianus is obviously writing before he knew of its destruction by bands of soldiers and monks in the late summer of 391) is compared to the Capitol, with which in another building metaphor Rome 'raises herself into eternity'; 'quo se venerabilis Roma in aeternum attollit' (22.16.12).

III

In his digression on Rome in Book 14, Ammianus had written of the achievement of the city in laying down laws, 'the foundation and eternal guarantees of liberty', before handing on her inheritance of power 'like a wise and thrifty parent' to the Caesars 'as to her children' (14.6.5). One aspect of the notion of Rome as the symbol of liberty emerges very plainly in the transition which I just mentioned, from Constantius' conduct on approaching Rome to his conduct once inside the city. Addressing the people and giving them equestrian races, he allowed himself to enjoy their traditional freedom, expressed in acclamations and reaching what in other circumstances might have been a dangerous outspokenness. Even the horse-races, of which in other cities, we are told, the emperor controlled the outcome, in Rome were allowed to proceed as chance and fortune allowed (16.10.14): a sort of physical enactment of the concept of perfect liberty (a little like the expression of the 'concept of extreme cold' with which Anthony Powell opens his cycle *Dance to the Music of Time*, as workmen round a brazier beat their arms together to keep warm). When, only four years after Constantius' visit the pretender Julian marched against him and justified his action in a letter to the senate, that body demanded in acclamations that he 'respect the author of his dignity'. This showed the senate, thought Ammianus, acting in the best traditions of its ancient frankness and confidence, *speciosa fiducia* (21.10.7).

Having described Rome as the founder of liberty by her making of laws, Ammianus departs in an interesting manner from a pattern of rhetorical interpretation that is so far rather predictable. The question of the role of liberty in relation to autocracy was, of course, the central question of the *Annals* of Tacitus, the reconciliation of *principatus* and *libertas*, as expressed in his *Agricola*, a conventional formulation of the relationship between senate and emperor under a benevolent government. Ammianus, however, writes not of conflict nor of mere reconciliation, but of a positive alliance between the two, achieved through the emperors' acceptance of an inheritance or birthright handed on to them by the senate.

The move in Ammianus' argument has two effects: first, it enables him to break out of the cycle of growth, old age and death to which his image of the development of Rome in terms of human life seems to have committed him. Ammianus is not talking, as a cursory reading might suggest, of a decline but of a rejuvenation of Rome in the persons and office of the emperors; it is through their efforts in conducting wars in the name of Rome ('nomine solo aliquotiens vincens') that Rome will 'live' — or 'conquer': *victura* — as long as there are men.

Second, Ammianus' placing of the defence of Rome and her values in the hands of the emperors conforms to the emphasis he places on their personal qualities, and to the role of human planning in the securing of the future. Criticising the conduct of the emperor Gratian in the year of the battle of Hadrianople, Ammianus reflects on the situation, which required an unremitting concentration on important issues, without the distraction of trivial forms of behaviour such as Commodus had indulged in (a severe comparison for the harmless Gratian!). Even had Marcus Aurelius been emperor, thought Ammianus, the situation could only with difficulty have been rescued, with the help of sensible colleagues and sober counsels; 'aegre sine collegis similibus et magna sobrietate consiliorum lenire luctuosos rei publicae poterat casus' (31.10.19). What is in practice meant by 'sobriety of counsel' comes out with harsh clarity in the aftermath of Hadrianople, when Julius, *magister militum* of the east, ordered to be assembled in the suburbs of the cities where they were stationed all the Goths presently in imperial service. The pretence was that they were to receive their pay, but in fact, once assembled, they were cut down to a man. To the modern mind the morality of this speaks for itself, but Ammianus would have seen such a reflection as a luxury, indeed as rather irresponsible. For him, the action of Julius saved the eastern provinces from disaster. It was a matter of 'effective action, quickly taken', 'efficacia... salutaris et velox'; a 'prudent counsel, quietly and promptly put into effect', 'quo consilio prudenti sine strepitu et mora completo...' (31.16.8).

From these examples, and indeed from the whole tenor of the history, it is clear that Ammianus attached the highest importance to the enterprise and physical energy which the emperors and their supporters invested in the protection of an empire entrusted to them by the senate. In a sensational scene in Ammianus, the emperor Valentinian actually died of a stroke, brought on by an explosion of pent-up anger while receiving an embassy of Quadi at Brigetio on the Danube (30.6.1–6). On a more mundane level, the emperors spent their lives marching back and forth along the frontiers where military challenges were set; like the Caesars of the Tetrarchy, in a phrase attributed to the emperor Constantius in a letter to Gallus Caesar, they devoted themselves to 'running here and there' — 'ultro citroque discurrentes' — in loyal obedience to their superiors' instructions (14.11.10).

The outstanding example, or rather the limiting case, of Ammianus' pattern is that of Julian. His early career in Gaul was marked for the extraordinary, and quite unexpected, military success that expelled the Alamanni to their lands beyond the Rhine, and for the equally remarkable reforms in administration and taxation which Julian achieved, often against his subordinates' advice: all as expressions of relentless personal energy, and of the conviction that by this, by discipline, and by constant intervention in the slow, recalcitrant processes of government, one could resist and turn back the tides of misfortune, mismanagement and corruption that had seemed endemic. More than this, one might even turn back the religious and cultural decline of the Constantinian era in favour of a renewal of the Golden Age of the Antonines. The Persian campaign, which a modern historian must regard as the most damaging possible legacy an emperor could leave to his successors, is presented by Ammianus as a continuation of the personal inspiration of Julian thwarted only (Ammianus is not at his happiest here, though he sets this theme at the centre of his account of the campaign) by the decrees of fate. If on this occasion the alliance of Virtue and Fortune that had made Rome great broke down, it was a failure of Fortune, for there was no doubt of Julian's virtue. The whole of Ammianus' obituary of Julian in Book 25 is designed in both content and structure to convey it.[12]

IV

Mention of Julian leads to an issue which from the point of view of the future, and therefore of this volume, is the most important issue of all: how, in his conception of the eternity of Rome, did Ammianus come to terms with Christianity? It is a real question, since (for example) Christianity is a notable absentee from the narrative of the visit of Constantius to Rome in 357. Only the old shrines and public places of Rome are mentioned, and these had indeed largely succeeded so far in excluding the physical presence of Christian churches from the centre of Rome.[13] But it is hard to believe that, in general, Constantius spent more time in the Forum and on the Capitol than he spent in the great Constantinian churches, especially St Peter's and St John Lateran.

It is worth recalling, too, that when Ammianus was completing his history at Rome in the later 380s, on the Ostia road outside the Aurelian walls of the city was being built a great church of St Paul. A *relatio* of Symmachus refers to it, a poem of Prudentius describes it, and it was dedicated by a Theodosian prefect of Rome in 391.[14] It has been shown in a new monograph on the Christian iconography of the later fourth century by J. M. Huskinson (most perceptively reviewed by David Hunt) how this is just the period, say 360–410, in which, with the encouragement of the papacy, Peter and Paul were being presented as the twin apostles of Rome, almost literally 'enshrining' the notion of Rome's foundation by Romulus and Remus as it was transferred to the new eternity represented now by Christianity.[15]

If there is a problem with this, as with other such interpretations of 'ideologies' in their literary and artistic representations, it is that of the extent of the public understanding of the often subtle patterns that were involved. As for this example, Ammianus is not surprisingly quite unaware of it. Not that his history neglects Christianity, far from it: his narrative is studded with allusions to the Christian church and its clergy, in a way that seems to me to do no serious disservice to their actual contribution to the events which Ammianus describes (their influence on matters he does *not* describe is of course a very different question). Though he obviously fails to represent the true proportion of their time which they devoted to the issue, Ammianus does mention religious belief and policy in nearly all his obituaries of emperors, in a way that pays at least formal acknowledgment to their importance.[16] He is not on all occasions hostile to the new religion, though clearly guarded in his attitude to its doctrines (and its technical vocabulary); he is capable, while reserving his position, of praising a modest provincial bishop and of expressing admiration for martyrs, and he refrains from polemic when it would, given a more openly polemical intention, have been very easy to indulge in it. It showed considerable restraint and honesty, for example, not to blame the bishop of Bezabde on the Tigris for revealing the weak points of the city's defences to the Persians, whose camp he had visited on an embassy (20.7.9).

Ammianus operates more subtly, by the displacement of Christianity from the position it believed itself to occupy, and by an irony that challenged its values, as I will try now to show.

In Book 15 (7.6ff.), Ammianus describes the attempt of Constantius to persuade Liberius of Rome to endorse the expulsion from his see of Athanasius of Alexandria. Athanasius was recalcitrant, and Constantius was eager to reinforce his own authority and that of ecclesiastical councils by that of the 'bishop of the eternal city'; 'auctoritate quoque potiore aeternae urbis episcopi' (15.7.10). Liberius refused to co-operate, and was himself exiled, being hustled out of the city by night for fear of the people, which 'burned with affection for him', 'qui eius amore flagrabat'. Ammianus' phrase 'auctoritate... aeternae urbis episcopi' has been taken, and one can see why, as an early attestation, in an unexpected source, of the principle of papal supremacy in the church. Despite the interesting fact that Ammianus is also the first writer of any sort to name the feast of Epiphany, there are many reasons why this interpretation cannot be correct.[17] Ammianus' description of the affair is notable for its sly 'secularisation' of the issues at stake. Athanasius has ideas 'above his profession', he dabbles in fortune-telling: Liberius is obstructive to the emperor, he is so popular that he has to be smuggled out to avert unrest in the city. The episode immediately follows the account, marvellously discussed by Erich Auerbach in his book *Mimesis*,[18] of the arrest, flogging and exile by the urban prefect Leontius of the riot leader Petrus Valvomeres — with a reference to his subsequent execution in Picenum for the rape of a 'young girl of a distinguished family': an interesting context in which to be writing of the authority of the 'bishop of the eternal city'! The riot led by Petrus had itself followed on from an earlier disorder over the arrest of a popular charioteer; and it is in this setting of persistent urban unrest that the episode of Liberius and Athanasius is told, and with the threat of its perpetuation that it closes. Whether intentionally or not (but surely intentionally), Ammianus is in this episode reminding us of the seamy side of life at Rome described in his earlier digression (in Book 14) Why was it that whenever his 'oratio' turned to Rome, nothing was found there to discuss except 'rioting, drunkenness and other such frivolities'? The conduct of Christians is indeed relevant to the life of the eternal city, but in its less savoury, more scandalous and trivial aspects.

The same consideration applies, as will be obvious, to the famous episode of the dissension between the supporters of Damasus and Ursinus over the succession to the see of St Peter. The outcome, 137 dead bodies on the floor of a Christian basilica, speaks for itself. Not that Ammianus will blame those who seek with such passion this great prize, 'considering the ostentation of urban life'. Successful candidates could grow rich on the donations of matrons, ride on grand carriages dressed in conspicuous clothes, and surpass the dinners of kings (27.3.14). Not only does Ammianus link the competition for the papacy with his theme of rioting and disorder at Rome; his description of the conduct in their high office of the ecclesiastical dignitaries of the city recalls nothing more vividly than his adverse account of the unworthy behaviour of Roman senators. These, too, paraded the streets of Rome, dressed in fine robes, which they lifted with gestures of their hands so as to reveal the beautifully embroidered undergarments (14.6.9). The similarity of conduct is enhanced when we compare Ammianus' descriptions with hostile letters of St Jerome on the worldly conduct of ambitious priests.[19]

Ammianus does indeed link Roman Christianity with the eternity of Rome, but only with that 'levitas paucorum incondita' which in the case of senators was the main threat to its values. In its connections with rioting and disorder, Ammianus robs the Christian faith of the motives integral to its own conduct; a subtle form of 'polemic by displacement' whereby, in further emphasising the ostentation of urban life as the chief motive of contenders for the papacy, he links Christianity with what, in his digression on Rome, is seen as most *un*worthy of the life and ideals of the city. Ammianus was not, when one compares him with writers like Eunapius of Sardis, a systematic propagandist against Christianity; but one cannot deny the skill with which he subverts the integrity and claims of urban Christianity, and so deprives it of a share, or at least a respectable share, in the future of the eternal city.

V

As I mentioned earlier, Ammianus' history is notable for the emphasis it places on the initiative, will and actions of the emperors — those emperors designated, as it were by 'legal' succession, as inheritors of the historical mission of Rome. It is this emphasis on the autonomy and effectiveness (*efficacia*) of the human will that seems to me above all to mark Ammianus as a Classical historian.

The contrast has often struck me between, in the next generation, the two writers Rutilius Namatianus and Orosius. For Rutilius, returning to Gaul in haste and at a dangerous time of year for sea travel, the crisis of the Roman empire was one to be met by human effort and enterprise. While his relative Exsuperantius suppressed a 'slave uprising' in Armorica, Rutilius returned late in 417 to the south-west to participate in Gallic politics in the aftermath of the recent Romano-Gothic alliance, upon the basis of which, one could hope, the political life of Gaul could be reconstructed. Jill Harries once taught me a lot by remarking simply on the first word of Rutilius' poem, *velocem*, 'rapid'; for the entire poem seems to convey, not at all the leisurely homecoming visualised by most of his critics, but urgency, haste and determination in a crisis.[20] Orosius, by contrast, in his precisely contemporary *Historia adversus paganos*, committed already to an interpretation of history in terms of the 'judgments of God', yields human initiative in favour of an acceptance of divine dispensation — an acceptance which accords ill with the outbursts of personal resentment expressed in some very striking passages tucked away in the largely unread earlier books of his history.[21]

In an article published in 1970 I argued similarly of the Greek historian of western affairs, Olympiodorus of Thebes, that he saw the failure of the western empire in the early fifth century as a failure of actual human policies in adverse circumstances provided largely by chance or Fortune, Τύχη; while the recovery, beginning with the installation of Valentinian III as emperor in 425, was based on the active intervention of the eastern court in his favour, as an expression of a restored unity in the Roman empire.[22] This unity was further pursued by the marriage of Valentinian to the eastern princess Eudoxia in 437, and by the compilation and publication, in that and the following year, of the Theodosian Code. Apart from the unity of east and west proclaimed by the actual process of compilation of the Code — that is to say the gathering of material from its scattered sources — what is the publication of a book of law except an assertion of confidence in the power of the effort and will of man in order to affect the circumstances that surround him? I do not find it a coincidence that the publication a century later of the Digest and Code of Justinian preceded the reconquest of the west, for both are statements of the confidence of a government; and so I read Ammianus' phrase that Rome 'will live as long as there are men' as much more than a rhetorical gesture. Nowhere is Ammianus more Classical in his perspectives, and at no point more superior to the unhappy Orosius, than in so connecting the eternity of Rome with the dimension of the human will and human effort.

NOTES

1. On the date of composition, see Alan Cameron, *JRS* 61 (1971), at 259–62 (reviewing Syme, *Ammianus and the Historia Augusta*). The latest extant reference in Ammianus is to the year 390 (26.5.14); several more are to the late 380s. The later date of publication often proposed involves assumptions relating to the historical (and especially the religious) background of the early 390s, but I see no need to ignore the explicit evidence in favour of untested hypothesis.
2. Libanius, *Ep.* 1063 Foerster, dated late 392, refers back to an earlier time — I would suggest to the stay of Theodosius and his supporters in the west, which ended in summer 391.
3. For some of the arguments on the structure and scope of Ammianus, see my 'Ammianus Marcellinus' in *Ancient Writers: Greece and Rome* (1982), II, 1117–38, at 1128: and 'Ammianus' historical evolution', in Brian Croke and Alanna Emmett (edd.), *History and Historians in Late Antiquity* (1983), 30–41, at 38. Both these articles are reprinted in *Political Life and Culture in Late Roman Society* (Variorum Reprints, 1985).
4. 'Pagan and Christian Historiography in the Fourth Century A.D.', in Momigliano (ed.), *The Conflict between Paganism and Christianity in the Fourth Century* (1963), 97 (= *Essays in Ancient and Modern Historiography* (1977), 122).
5. See for this point and what follows my 'Ammianus Marcellinus', 1121–4, and 'Ammianus' historical evolution', 31–3.
6. 'Ammianus Marcellinus', 1125–7; 'Ammianus' historical evolution', 34–9.
7. I accept in essentials W.R. Chalmers, 'Eunapius, Ammianus Marcellinus and Zosimus on Julian's Persian Expedition', *CQ* n.s. 10 (1960), 152–60; cf. T.D. Barnes, *The Sources of the Historia Augusta* (Coll. Latomus 155, 1978), 117–20 — while feeling that closer attention should be paid to Ammianus' specific purpose in the passages in which his reliance upon Eunapius seems demonstrable.
8. Francois Paschoud, *Roma Aeterna: Etudes sur le patriotisme romain dans l'occident latin à l'époque des grandes invasions* (1967), esp. at 59–67.
9. For Ammianus' notices, with the supporting evidence, A. Chastagnol, *Les Fastes de la Préfecture de Rome au Bas-Empire* (1962).
10. Sabine MacCormack, *Art and Ceremony in Late Antiquity* (1981), esp. 17–61.
11. Frag. 43 Muller (= 41.1 Blockley). See my 'Olympiodorus of Thebes and the history of the west (A.D. 407–425)', *JRS* 60 (1970), 79–97, esp. 80. Also in Variorum Reprints (above, n. 3).
12. Above, n. 6. The obituary (25.4.1–27) is arranged under the four cardinal virtues, 'ut sapientes definiunt', followed by 'external virtues', 'eisque accedentes extrinsecus aliae', etc. This differs from the structure of any other imperial obituary in Ammianus, and is clearly framed as a panegyric.

13. R. Krautheimer, *Rome: Profile of a City, 312–1308* (1980), esp. 29ff.
14. Chastagnol, *Fastes*, No. 96, F1. Philippus (pp. 238–9), presents the administrative evidence but does not mention the description of the church offered by Prudentius, *Peristephanon* xii 45–54.
15. J.M. Huskinson, *Concordia Apostolorum. Christian Propaganda at Rome in the Fourth and Fifth Centuries; a Study in Christian Iconography and Iconology* (BAR International Series 148, 1982); E.D. Hunt, *JRS* 74 (1984), 229–31. The theme was explored by Ch. Piétri, 'Concordia Apostolorum et renovatio urbis', *MEFR* 73 (1961), 273–322, and in his *Roma Christiana: Recherches sur l'église de Rome, son organisation, sa politique, son idéologie, de Miltiade à Sixte III (311–440)* (Bibl. de l'Ecole française d'Athènes et de Rome 284, 1976) II, Chap. 18, esp. 1583ff. (I do not know whether it is inevitable that books on this subject should produce such long titles).
16. See esp. E.D. Hunt, 'Christians and Christianity in Ammianus Marcellinus', *CQ* n.s. 35 (1985), 186–200.
17. Hunt, 190; cf. 188 for Epiphany (Amm. 21.2.5). I am less sure about the tonsure (Hunt, 193; Amm. 22.11.9).
18. *Mimesis: the Representation of Reality in Western Literature* (1953, repr. 1968), 50–76.
19. D.S. Wiesen, *St Jerome as a Satirist* (1964).
20. See my *Western Aristocracies and Imperial Court*, A.D. *364–425* (1975), at 325–8. My view of Rutilius is in general terms confirmed by the content of the new fragment published by M. Ferrari, *Italia Medioevale e Umanistica* 16 (1973), 12ff.
21. For Orosius and the 'Judgments of God', see Santo Mazzarino, *The End of the Ancient World* (Eng. tr. 1966), 58–76 (with substantial exaggeration of Orosius' intellectual merits).
22. *JRS* 60 (1970), at 80, 97.

III

CHRONICLE AND THEOLOGY: PROSPER OF AQUITAINE

R.A. Markus

Prosper has suffered from a double handicap: from being seen, in respect of his theological work, inevitably, in the shadow of Saint Augustine; and, perhaps less inevitably, from being seen in the shadow of Mommsen's withering judgment on his historical competence. 'In sum', so Mommsen wrote in the introduction to his edition of the *Chronicle*, 'it would hardly be possible to write a book with less care and exactitude than this Aquitanian's production'.[1] Yet, Prosper remains one of the most influential of fifth-century writers. His *Chronicle* was used within two years of its completion by Victorius of Aquitaine for the consular lists of his own *cursus paschalis*; Cassiodorus took the information he used for the years from 379 to 455 in his *Chronicle* from a version of Prosper's; the African writers Liberatus of Carthage and Victor of Tonnenna in the middle of the sixth century knew and made use of his work (though the latter under the name of Lucentius). It would be tiresome to survey later historians from the anonymous chroniclers who incorporated Prosper's *Chronicle* in their own 'chronographical productions'[2] to historians such as Paul the Deacon who made use of it.

Prosper was no less influential as the leader of the theological opposition to the reaction against the extreme forms of Augustine's teaching on grace and predestination. This reaction, centred on the monasteries of Marseille and Lerins and articulated primarily by John Cassian, called forth a series of works of theological controversy from Prosper's pen. An anthology of Augustinian *Sententiae* and a collection of comments on the last part of the Psalter, based on Augustine's, or drawn from them with varying degrees of fidelity to their original, have also come down to us.[3] A work entitled *The call of all nations* has long been dubious, but its attribution to Prosper is now widely accepted. To this we shall have to return later.

The *Chronicle* is Prosper's only historical work. Its authenticity is not in doubt, but a number of puzzles about it remain. Mommsen has demonstrated[4] the carelessness — even the 'fraudulence' — with which Prosper treats the dates he derived from consular lists; and the dates of his entries in the later part of the *Chronicle*, where Prosper is writing about his own times, need careful controlling. With problems of this kind

I cannot deal here. I shall keep to one central cluster of questions raised by a reading of the *Chronicle*: the relation between the composition of the work and Prosper's career. As I shall indicate, this question will take us into a discussion of the relationship between Prosper and Pope Leo I, and, in the end, into some consideration of the wider questions concerning Prosper's historical and theological objectives.

Gennadius in his catalogue of famous men reported of Prosper that he was thought to have composed Pope Leo's letters against Eutyches.[5] We shall need to scrutinise this statement, but we must first consider the prior question it raises, in so far as it is, at least on the face of it, evidence that Prosper moved from his native Gaul to Rome at some point in his career. The composition of the *Chronicle* appears to confirm this supposition. The work has come down to us in a number of different editions.[6] The recension continued by Victor of Tonnenna ended not in 455, the year when Prosper finally left off writing, but in 443, and other manuscript traditions suggest editions which went down to 445 or 451. The most significant break, however, occurs after the entry for the year 433 (between nos. 1311 and 1319). The chronological summaries which appear at this point correspond in form to those found at the end of Jerome's *Chronicle*, which Prosper used for the period it covered, ending with 379. This point marks a formal break in the post-Hieronymian part of Prosper's *Chronicle*, a clear indication that an earlier edition had ended at this point. On the basis of this caesura important inferences have been made concerning Prosper's career.

If we assume, on the basis of Gennadius' report, that Prosper left Gaul to take up residence in Rome, as it would be reasonable to assume, then this break in the *Chronicle* would both confirm this and suggest that he did so soon after 433. Most scholars have in fact taken this as evidence for both Prosper's move and for its date. Dom Cappuyns, for instance, wrote in 1929 that Prosper's departure for Rome 'is indicated by an examination of the *Chronicle*' — and here he referred to an article by Hauck in the *Protestantische Realkenzyklopaedie* neatly sandwiched between 'Proselyten' and 'Protestanten' — 'Whatever may be the case with successive redactions, a new part [of the *Chronicle*] begins in 434–435, from which point Gaul suddenly gives way to Rome, both for interest and for information'.[7] Mommsen, writing in 1892, had, with characteristic acumen, expressed scepticism; but Cappuyns's view has been generally accepted, usually without question.[8]

It is worth reopening this question, not so much in order to decide whether Prosper moved to Rome and if so when, but for the light that may thereby be thrown on two related questions. First: what exactly is the relation between Prosper's (alleged, indeed likely) move to Rome in mid-Chronicle and the *Chronicle* itself? Does the work really provide the evidence it has been made to provide of a shift in interest and point of view? Second: what is the nature of the relationship between Prosper and Leo, with whom Gennadius associates Prosper to the extent of making him his notary and reporting — though on the strength of no more than hearsay, as he is careful to tell us — that Prosper was thought to have been the author of the pope's letters against the Eutychian heresy? There is no good reason to doubt that Prosper did go to Rome. But it must be said that the alleged evidence for this from the *Chronicle* — the difference between the parts of the work preceding and following the break after 433 — is non-existent. I can find no sign of the alleged Rome-ward shift in both 'interest' and 'information'.[9] 'Interest' and 'information' are not easy to assess in objective or quantitative fashion; but for what numbers are worth here, on my reckoning not more than one in five entries refer to Gaul in the section of the *Chronicle* devoted to the years from 379 to 433, and the proportion is much the same in the later section covering the years from 434 to 455. (I count *at most* 19 out of 98 entries in the first, and *at least* 4 out of 22 in the second part; I omit the consular headings for each year in my count.) Prosper's interest in Gaul, in both sections, falls into a general pattern of interest in the affairs of the Western Empire — Gaul, Britain, Spain and, especially, Vandal North Africa.

If his attention to Gaul fails to indicate a shift in his point of view, can we detect its alleged obverse, a greater interest in and better knowledge of Roman matters, in the later section? The case here is somewhat stronger. There is certainly no lack of interest in Roman and especially papal matters, and particularly in Pope Leo, in this last part of the *Chronicle*. But we must not jump to hasty conclusions from this. A comparison with some entries in the earlier section is revealing. Under the year 429 (n.1301) Prosper was able to tell us about Pope Celestine sending Germanus to Britain to combat heresy, and even to reveal to us the source of the advice on which the Pope acted.[10] A few entries later (n.1307) he gives us inside information on the same pope's reasons for sending Palladius to minister to Irish Christians. Good information, on any reckoning; and Prosper could have got it only from Roman sources. It might be argued, of course, that this is the sort of information he would have obtained after settling in Rome, and that he could have inserted it into revised versions of the earlier part of his work when working on the later editions; we cannot tell, for no MS tradition preserves the first edition in its original state. It seems far easier to suppose, however, and far likelier, that he received his information about Pope Celestine — and what else we can only guess — at the time of a visit he is known to have made to Rome with a deacon Hilary in 431–2 in the hope of obtaining the pope's support for his campaign against Augustine's detractors in Southern Gaul.[11] That this was in fact the case is suggested by a brief allusion to Celestine's concern about Britain and about Ireland that Prosper made in a work written very soon after his return to Gaul.[12] The information, clearly, was available to Prosper before 433; the likelihood is that he inserted it into his *Chronicle* then, though it is not impossible that he revised the work when he settled in Rome, or even that he composed all of it there.

To summarise: there is no reason for doubting Prosper's attachment to the Roman see and his interest in the doings of its occupants, both surely enhanced by his visit to Pope Celestine, which must have given him a new circle of contacts and new information. Equally, there is no reason to doubt that he settled in Rome at some time after 433. But there is nothing in the *Chronicle* which would suggest a shift in the focus of Prosper's interest or any decisive change in the nature of the sources of information available to him between writing the two parts.

To come to our second question, concerning the relationship between Prosper and Pope Leo. Gennadius' statement associating the two men could well be true; it could equally well be the result of Gennadius, or his informants, putting two and two together to make a sum well in excess of four. Prosper was known to be the author of a collection of papal and other documents dug out of Roman archives;[13] he was known to have interested himself in the christological controversies raging in Leo's time;[14] and both admiration for Leo and a fair knowledge of his activities could easily be inferred from the text of the *Chronicle*. Put together, this medley of evidence could have led Gennadius or his informants to the plausible conjecture that Prosper — especially if he was known to have taken up residence in Rome — had become Leo's secretary. It need not be wrong, even if it is all very uncertain. Does the *Chronicle* itself, taken together with other evidence, allow us to specify the nature of the link between Prosper and Leo with any more certitude?

From the year 439 onwards Leo is frequently mentioned in the *Chronicle*, first as deacon, then as pope (nn. 1336[?], 1341, 1350, 1358, 1367, 1369, 1378). Prosper is well-informed on Leo and admired him, to the extent that good modern scholars have drawn inferences falling not far short of Gennadius'. Prosper is said, for instance, to have greeted Leo's advent in Rome 'with real enthusiasm';[15] or, 'In every word we can recognise the papal servant, indeed the pope's secretary'.[16] Now there is nothing in the *Chronicle* that would authorise conclusions as specific as that. To turn evidence for the proximity of the two men into something more definite, two other kinds of evidence have been adduced. The first consists of a number of similarities between some of Prosper's and some of Leo's views and expressions. This question is of fundamental importance for my present enquiry, and I postpone it for discussion in some detail later. The other kind of grounds on which Prosper is inferred specifically to have had some part in the composition of some of Leo's letters, either as their first drafter, or as their final editor, or in some other collaborative capacity, rests on an examination of Leo's correspondence. This we need now, briefly, to consider.

Carlo Silva-Tarouca has distinguished among the groups of manuscripts of Leo's letters a group which is marked off from the rest by its stylistic features, especially by greater expertise shown in these letters in the use of the traditional rules of epistolary *cursus*.[17] I am unable to comment on this, but the conclusion has the weight of Silva-Tarouca's authority, and apparently cogent argumentation behind it. This cannot, however, be said of the next step in the argument, in which this unknown papal notary is simply identified, on the strength of Gennadius's report, with Prosper. A more specific attempt to prove that Leo's Tome to Flavian, patriarch of Constantinople, on Christ's two natures was written by Prosper is based on some rather ill-defined features held to be distinctive of Prosper and of Leo respectively: for instance that the Tome displays a severity against heresy more characteristic of Prosper than of Leo. I can attach little weight to this, and no more to the only specific argument deployed to this end, to the effect that the term *substantia*, common in Leo's sermons but avoided by Prosper, is also absent from the Tome.[18] This argument would have force if it were less easy to think of good reasons why Leo might have wished to avoid using this term in such a document.[19] We shall return to other similarities found between passages of Leo's sermons and Prosper's *Chronicle* which have sometimes been invoked as evidence for Prosper as Leo's secretary.[20] Similarities there undoubtedly are, and, as I shall suggest, they are of great importance; but they do not underpin Gennadius' report.

For these similarities it is very easy to account without turning Prosper into a papal secretary, simply by observing that Prosper had already been given access to Roman archives in 431–2 (see n.11) and that we may safely accept that he continued to have such access later on, at a time when he was probably living in Rome, perhaps as the pope's friend. There are several entries in the *Chronicle* which seem to reflect a knowledge of Leo's correspondence: thus the entry for the year 443 (n.1350) in which Prosper reports Leo's drive against the Manichees in Rome points to Leo's *Ep*.7 and *Sermo* 16; his report under the year 453 (n.1369) on the Council of Chalcedon could be, though it need not be, based on the pope's correspondence concerning the matter of Eutyches and its sequel from the Council of 449 to Chalcedon in 451; and the very last entry in the *Chronicle* (n.1376) contains explicit mention of known letters written by Pope Leo (Ballerini, *Epp*. 121, 137 and 142) in connection with the controversy over the date of Easter, a matter on which Prosper is not unreasonably thought to have had some interest.[21] Historians as great as Bede and, following him, Erich Caspar, have inferred collaboration between the two men.[22] We may, at any rate, accept that Prosper knew of the pope's concerns in these matters, and, being on friendly terms with him, shared them, and was in a position to obtain information without difficulty.

I come now to the last section of my enquiry, the question of Leo's influence on Prosper in his later years, and the light that it might cast on Prosper's historical interests. I want to suggest that rather than looking for traces of Prosper's hand in Leo's letters — traces which may or may not be there — we should see Prosper in the later part of his career as strongly under Pope Leo's influence: a theological influence which left some imprint on Prosper's historical thought. In his theological works Prosper came closest to reflecting on history in his *The Calling of all nations*: a meditation, in the light of the controversies he had engaged in for perhaps as long as some twenty years, on the mystery of God's election and human salvation. Doubts, serious and long held, have been largely laid to rest by Dom Cappuyns's defence of its Prosperian authorship.[23] It is still rewarding, however, to consider one group of the arguments which have been deployed against attributing the work to Prosper since the end of the seventeenth century. The many close resemblances to be found between the text of this work and Pope Leo's letters and sermons furnished one of the strongest grounds on which Pasquier Quesnel ascribed the work to Leo.[24] In their classic *Observationes* on *Quesnel's* second *Dissertatio* the Ballerini brothers, though they remained unable to identify the author of the *De vocatione*, decisively disposed of the alleged proofs of Leonine authorship. The resemblances were the result of Leo's influence on the author. Dom Cappuyns rounded off their conclusions by establishing the work as Prosper's.[25] The passages adduced as evidence for Leonine authorship have thus turned into examples of Leo's influence on Prosper, and we must consider them in order to gauge its nature and extent.

First, however, it is important to pause for a moment to consider the extraordinariness of the circumstances in which Prosper came under Leo's influence. It is very likely that the two men became acquainted long before Leo became pope, while he was a Roman deacon: probably at the time of the visit to Rome made by Prosper and Hilary in 431–2.[26] Their arch-enemy, John Cassian, was, however, at this time, 'on the best of terms'[27] with the Roman see and its archdeacon, Leo; and it was Cassian who, at Leo's request, wrote a theological statement on the Nestorian heresy for Western consumption. At the beginning of his preface to this tract Cassian took care to remind Leo that he had other theological attainments behind him, indeed, quite specifically, his *Collations*:[28] the very work Prosper and his friends found so objectionable. This was not a moment at which Prosper and Hilary could count on unambiguous support from Rome against the 'Collator'; and they did not get it in pope Celestine's 'evasive' response to their request.[29] Leo's influence in helping to prevent a deep and lasting split between Cassian and Prosper and their followers deserves some emphasis. If Leo's influence did not, at this stage, in the early 430s, cool Prosper's anti-Cassianic fervour, we might expect it to have left a mark at least on the later stages of Prosper's work. Since Cappuyns's study it has been generally agreed that the development of Prosper's thought is marked by a less rigid expression of the extreme forms of Augustinian views on predestination, and by a greater stress on the universality of God's saving will.[30] Now if there is one feature in Leo's thought that stands out and might be expected to have left a mark on Prosper's work, it is his universalism. If there is a second such theme, it would be the Rome-centredness of Leo's universalistic outlook. For it was Leo who drew together the threads of a christianised version — which had been taking shape over something like the previous half century — of the ancient Rome ideology.

Among the passages noted by Quesnel as strikingly leonine in character there is one particularly interesting in this connection. A crucial chapter of the *De vocatione* (II.16) is headed 'That Christ died for all'. It is a straightforward re-statement of the classic images of the universality of salvation offered by Christ in the Church: it mentions the Pentecostal assembly of nations who heard the Gospel proclaimed each in its own tongue, and the subsequent spread of the message far and wide among the more distant nations. At this point in the chapter the author adds two significant codas. These, together, constitute the passage Quesnel had noted as paralleled in a sermon preached by Leo on a feast of Saints Peter and Paul (*Sermo* 82). Prosper's first coda runs:

> We believe that the sway and extension of the Roman Empire had been prepared by God's providence to this end, that the nations which were called to the unity of Christ's Body were first to be gathered under the authority of one Empire.

This idea is, of course, an old common-place going back to Eusebius, Origen, and, beyond them, even to the second century. In the course of the fourth century it became one of the most ubiquitous of the clichés in which the history of the Roman Empire and of the Christian Church came to be seen. Leo's sermon contained a fine re-statement of the idea,[31] and his words may well have been in Prosper's mind when he wrote this chapter. The very last sentence of the chapter, rounding off the second of his codas (which I will consider in a moment) sounds like pure Leo:

> Rome has become greater as the citadel of religion by her *principatus* of the apostolic priesthood than she had ever been as the seat of power.

It is certainly not hard to understand why Quesnel should have attributed a work containing such words to Leo.

But we have not considered Prosper's second coda, the passage immediately following the first (see above) which ends with this leonine statement on Rome. It is of the utmost importance in trying to understand the way Prosper's mind worked, and it is worth quoting in full:

> However (*quamvis*: a significant connective here): the grace of Christianity is not content to have the boundaries of Rome as its limits; for it has submitted to the sceptre of Christ's cross many peoples whom Rome could not subject with its arms [and then follows the leonine conclusion we have already quoted]: Rome has become greater as the citadel of religion by her *principatus* of the apostolic priesthood than it ever was as the seat of power.

This is a remarkable passage, for in it Prosper goes out of his way — and out of his way gratuitously, for no one could have taken Leo's words as implying any confining of the Gospel within the Roman boundaries — to dissociate himself from a view which he had found in one of the chief sources he used in writing his *Chronicle*: Orosius' *Seven books against the pagans*.[32] Orosius had, notoriously, used the cliché of the providential coincidence of Christianity and the Roman Empire as a way of reconciling the barbarian invasions of the early fifth century with his own band of historical optimism (VIII.41):

> We ought to praise God's mercy, which has contrived to bring the nations, even at the cost of our [i.e. Roman] weakness, to the knowledge of so great a truth, which might otherwise have remained inaccessible to them.

We can be sure that Prosper had read Orosius. Moreover, this particular passage had evidently made quite an impression on him for a few pages later in the same work (II.31) he once again alludes to it, this time deliberately balancing the christianisation of the barbarians settled in Roman territory with a remark on the conversion of barbarians living beyond the Roman boundaries by their Roman slaves. (We might be inclined to think this somewhat lame; but it seems that for genuine missionary activity initiated by Roman clergy we look in vain until the sixth century.[33]) Prosper is clearly anxious to distance himself from Orosius' view, a widely current commonplace of his age, that the Empire was the 'container' of Christendom, its boundaries limiting its extent and its accessibility. In this respect at least Prosper was Augustine's true disciple.[34]

Prosper's procedure in these two codas, then, can only be reconstructed as follows: (i) He began with an exposition of the universality of salvation; the spread of the faith through the simultaneous translation at Pentecost and subsequent broadcast to all nations, first near, then far. This is the kernel of his argument and forms part of the core of his book. (ii) He went on to the providential assistance afforded by the Empire to the spread of Christianity, an idea he found in the sermon of Leo's he was echoing, but a commonplace he had also come across in Orosius (and, perhaps, elsewhere). (iii) Remembering the way Orosius had used this *topos*, Prosper realised that it could undermine his argument: if the Empire was the vehicle of the Gospel and coextensive with Christianity, was the universality of grace not restricted by the Empire's boundaries? (iv) No; this could not be; and, luckily, it was Leo himself who provided the exit from Prosper's dilemma.

Preaching to his Roman congregation on the feast day of the Roman church's apostolic patrons, Leo apostrophised Rome as a 'holy people, an elect nation, a priestly and royal city, become, through Saint Peter's see established here, the head of the world (*caput orbis*), ruling more widely now by means of divine religion than it ever did by worldly dominion' (*Sermo* 82.1). Leo was rounding off the theme of the *renovatio urbis* through its rebirth in the faith of its founding apostles.[35] The old myth of Rome had come to serve as a symbol of Rome's renewal, her waning power translated into truly universal dominion by the apostolic re-founders of the City. This is the universalism which rescued Prosper from the fetters that Orosius' vision of Roman and Christian history would have placed on grace: a parochialism he now saw as more restricting than the rigid Augustinianism he had defended against John Cassian.

To return, finally, to the subject of this enquiry, the *Chronicle*: I have used it this far only for the light it casts on the author's career. I end with the question: what if any light does the author's career throw on the *Chronicle*? The answer is, not much. A few entries, especially those relating to 'missions' to Pelagian Britain and heathen Ireland could be taken as exemplifying Prosper's concern to uphold the universality of the call to all nations. Similarly, the strongly Rome-centred character of Prosper's universalism is well represented and needs no special illustration. We have already noticed the abundant entries devoted to Leo and his work, and to these we may add the references to his predecessors, especially Pope Celestine. Prosper's interest in the papacy emerges progressively more sharply focussed on the *principatus* of Rome's apostolic priesthood, which, as he said in the *De vocatione*,[36] has made Rome greater — especially now, with Leo's achievement — 'than she had been as the seat of power'. Such themes are naturally of interest to Prosper the historian as well as to Prosper the theologian, and he duly alludes to them in the appropriate places in the *Chronicle*. It is equally unsurprising to find many entries relating to heresy, especially Pelagianism, and the fight against it. Many entries in *Chronicle* echo anticipations of these themes in his earlier writings.[37] This is not a large harvest, and it reveals nothing unexpected.

If we were to ask the larger question: why did Prosper, with most of his life devoted to theological controversy, write a *Chronicle*?, we would have to be content with guesswork for any answers. One guess would be the example of Jerome. Prosper wrote his *Chronicle* — as did some more conscientious practitioners of the craft — as a continuation of Jerome's. He also well knew the part Jerome had played in the fight against Pelagius: 'in his most excellent books he dissected the enemy and showed with what storm-clouds the newly risen darkness threatened to obscure the true light'.[38] Prosper's admiration for his great precursor as a hammer of the Pelagians might well have led him to continue Jerome's historical as well as his theological labours. He failed to follow the example Jerome had set him of care over questions of chronology and accuracy in the use of sources (happily, he also failed to follow Jerome's examples of slanderous virulence against his enemies). What is most remarkable about the *Chronicle*, however, is the range and variety of material, the comparative wealth of the information it gives us, for instance about Aetius' activities in Gaul, the Vandals' in Africa, of treaties of settlement made by the government with the Goths and the Vandals, and other wholly secular matters with no relation to Prosper's theological interests. Often it is information given us by no other source. The history of Valentinian III's reign would contain many more, and much larger, blanks than it does if we had to do without Prosper.

The figure Prosper would have been most conscious of as the chief inspiration of his work would unquestionably have been Augustine. From him Prosper could certainly have derived a sense of history as the theatre of God's hidden purposes. But it can only have been his own awareness of the dramatic material furnished by the history of his own times, the second quarter of the fifth century, and his closeness to some of the central protagonists in the great scenes, that turned that sense of history into chronicle record. Prosper's interest in history seems to go back a long way: *rerum gestarum relationes*, he had written, perhaps about the time when he had just completed the first part of his *Chronicle*, 'historical narratives' were among the things which drew men's minds to the contemplation of God.[39] The chapter containing this remark is based on one of Augustine's finest sermons;[40] but the remark is Prosper's addition. Augustine had said not a word about historical narratives in this sermon (nor, for that matter, about the beauty of the created order, except under the inclusive 'delight in the truth'). But, for all that, Prosper's addition lay along the theological grain of the *City of God*.[41]

NOTES

1. *Chronica minora* 1 (*MGH AA* 9, Berlin, 1892) 348.
2. The phrase is quoted from B. Croke and A.M. Emmett, 'Historiography in Late Antiquity: an overview', in *History and historians in Late Antiquity*, ed. Croke and Emmett (Sydney, 1983) 1–12, at p.4. The essay is a very felicitous summary of the nature of the *genre*.
3. The best summary is D.M. Cappuyns, 'Le premier représentant de l'augustinisme médiéval, Prosper d'Aquitaine', *RTAM* 1 (1929) 307–337. Cf. also the introductions by P.De Letter to his translations of Prosper, *The call of all nations* (ACW 14, Westminster, Maryland, 1952) and *Defense of St. Augustine*, (ACW 32, 1963); R. Lorenz, 'Der Augustinismus Prospers von Aquitanien', *ZKG*, 73 (1962) 217–252. Lorenz's conclusion (at p. 225) that Prosper's *Expositio* must originally have embraced the whole Psalter has been called into question by the latest editor of the work, P. Callens, in the introduction to his edition: see CC 68A (Turnholt, 1972) viii, n.3.
4. loc.cit. (above, n.1), 352.
5. Gennadius, *Der vir.ill.*, 85: *ab ipso dictatae creduntur*.
6. Mommsen's summary: *loc.cit.* (n.1 above), 345.
7. Cappuyns, *loc.cit.* (above, n.3), 326 n.45, referring to A. Hauck, 'Prosper von Aquitanien', *RE* 16/3 (1905) 123–127, at 126.
8. See for example, De Letter (cf.above, n.3), *The call*, 9–10, and *Defense*, 12 with n.45; cf.G. Bardy in *DTC* 13/1 (Paris, 1936) 846–850, at 847. G. de Plinval, 'Prosper d'Aquitaine, interprète de saint Augustin', *Rech.aug.* 1 (1958) 339–355 assumes (343), without evidence or argument, that Prosper was taken back to Rome by Leo on his return from his visit to Gaul at the time of his election to the see of Rome. T. Hodgkin, *Italy and her invaders*, I/2 (Oxford, 1892) 707, thought Prosper's move to Rome to be 'probable', and dated it to *c.* 440. Mommsen: *loc.cit.* (above, n.1), 344.
9. Cf. above, n.7. O. Holder-Egger, 'Die Chronik Prospers von Aquitanien', *Neues Archiv* 1 (1876) 15–90; 327–334 adduces grounds for thinking that the *Chronicle* was known in Rome by 449, and that its last part must have been, and the whole probably was, in Holder-Egger's opinion, composed there (see 44–45).
10. On this see now E.A. Thompson, *Saint Germanus of Auxerre and the end of Roman Britain* (Studies in Celtic history, VI, Woodbridge, Suffolk, 1984) 29–30, 79–80.
11. For the date — between June 431 and July 432 — see Cappuyns, *loc.cit.* (above, n.3) 318–319, n.26.
12. *C.Coll.* 21.2 It is noteworthy that here Prosper suggests (as he does not in the *Chronicle*) that the purpose of the Irish mission was conversion: *dum Romanam insulam studet servare catholicam, fecit etiam barbaram christianam*. The evidently rhetorical character of this statement inclines me to place more weight on the sober entry in the *Chronicle* (1307) according to which Palladius was sent as the first bishop *ad Scottos in Christo credentes*.

13. On the authorship of the *Capitula*, see D.M. Cappuyns, 'L'origine des capitula pseudo-célestiens', *RB* 41 (1929) 156–170.
14. Prosper is apt to associate Nestorian with Pelagian heresy: *C.Coll.*21.2; cf. *Epit.,PL* 51.153–4; *Chron.* 1306 On this, see O. Chadwick, *John Cassian*, 2nd ed. (Cambridge, 1968) 142–143.
15. R. Helm, 'Prosper', in *PW* XXIII (1957) 880–897 at 895–6; cf. L.Valentin, *S.Prosper d'Aquitaine*, (Toulouse, 1900) 195; on the *Chronicle*, see pp. 195–204 and 411–441.
16. Holder-Egger, *loc.cit.* (above, n.9) 66. Cf. n.21 below.
17. 'Nuovi studi sulle lettere dei papi', *Gregorianum* 12 (1931) 547–598, at 571–2.
18. J. Gaidioz, 'Saint Prosper d'Aquitaine et le Tome à Flavien', *RSR* 23 (1949) 270–301.
19. H. Arens, *Die christologische Sprache Leos des Grossen. Analyse des Tomus an den Patriarchen Flavian* (Freiburger theologische Studien, 122. Freiburg, 1982) 315f. notes Leo's increasingly consistent avoidance of the term *substantia*.
20. See N. Ertl, 'Diktatoren frühmittelalterlicher Papstbriefen', *Arch.f. Urkundenforsch.* 15 (1938) 56–132, at 57–61.
21. Ertl, *ibid.*; cf. Holder-Egger, *loc.cit.* (above, n.9) 67.
22. Bede, *De rat.temp.* 43, presumably based on Marcellinus Comes and Gennadius and Prosper's *Chronicle*. Caspar, *Geschichte des Papsttums* I (Tübingen, 1930) 460 and 546.
23. 'L'auteur du De vocatione omnium gentium', *RB* 39 (1927) 198–226. For a survey of subsequent views, see Lorenz, *loc.cit.* (above, n.3) 233, n.129. See, however, Plinval, *loc.cit.* (above, n.8) 352. The dating of the work, however, remains uncertain: Lorenz (following an unpublished thesis by Gaidioz which I have not been able to consult) inclines to *c.*440 rather than the date favoured by Cappuyns and most others, *c.*450.
24. P. Quesnel, *Dissertatio secunda, De auctore librorum de vocatione omnium gentium* (Lyon, 1700), reprinted by the Ballerini brothers in *Sancti Leonis Magni romani pontificis Opera* (Venice, 1756), tom.2: Diss.II: 615–660. See especially *c.*15 (625) for a summary of the reasons for the attribution; 19 (628–630) for parallels in the use of Scripture; 20 (630–633) on doctrinal similarities, and 21 (633–635) on individual parallel passages.
25. Ballerini, *loc.cit.* (preceding note) *c.*21 and Cappuyns, *loc.cit.* (above, n.23) 221–225.
26. See above, n.11. On it, Valentin, *op.cit.* (above, n.15) 135.
27. O. Chadwick, *op.cit.* (above, n.14) 131.
28. *De Inc., Praef.* (*CSEL* 17. 235).
29. Cf. Cappuyns, *loc.cit.* (above, n.3) 318–319, 326–327; 'evasive': 326. Cf. Chadwick, *op.cit.* (above, n.14) 132.
30. Cappuyns, *loc.cit.* (above, n.3) esp. 327–337; De Letter, *Call*, 164–165, n.52; and Plinval, *loc.cit.* (above, n.8) 351–352. For an important reservation to the view that Prosper's later work represents a substantial retreat from the Augustinian position, see Lorenz, *loc.cit.* (above, n.3) 237–251.
31. *Sermo* 82.2: *Ut autem hujus inenarrabilis gratiae per totum mundum diffunderetur effectus, Romanum regnum divina providentia praeparavit...*
32. Holder-Egger, *loc.cit.* (above, n.9) 88 on Prosper's use of Orosius VII.42 in his entry for 411; Valentin, *op.cit.* (above, n.15) 427 on his misunderstanding of Oros. VII.37 in n.1218.
33. I still accept this view, defended by E.A. Thompson, 'Christianity and the Northern barbarians', *Nott.med.st.* 1 (1957) 3–21, repr.in *The conflict between paganism and Christianity in the fourth century*, ed. A.D. Momigliano (Oxford, 1963) 56–78. Cf. n.12, above.
34. On Augustine (and Orosius) see my *Saeculum: History and society in the theology of Saint Augustine* (Cambridge, 1970) 39–40 and 161–162. Peter Brown's jibes (see his *Augustine of Hippo* (London, 1967) 401) against Augustine who 'was concerned to

explain away' (referring to *De corr. et gr.*, 14.44) the statement that 'God wishes all men to be saved' (I Tim.2.4) and against Prosper, who is said 'to treat it as a "trite objection"' (in his *Ep.ad Ruf.* 13.14) are an uncharacteristic caricature of their views. Two interesting versions of Roman dominion extending beyond the frontiers: Sidonius Apollinaris, *Epp.*II.1.4 and IV.17.2.

35. On this theme see E.H. Kantorowicz, '*Puer exoriens*: On the Hypapante mosaics of S. Maria Maggiore', *Perennitas: Beiträge zur christlichen Archäologie und Kunst...* *P.Th.Michels*, ed. H. Rahner & E. von Severus (Münster, 1963) 118–135, repr. in his *Selected studies* (New York, 1965) 25–36; Ch.Pietri, 'Concordia apostolorum et renovatio urbis', *MEFR* 73 (1961) 275–322, and his *Roma cristiana* (*BEFA&R* 224, Rome 1976) Livre III. On Leo, see P.A. McShane, *La romanitas et le pape Léon le Grand* (Tournai & Montreal, 1979) 53–232.

36. *De voc.* II.16 (see above); *Carm.de Ingr.* 39–42.

37. E.g. *Chron.* nn. 1252 (cf. *Ingr.* 13, 26, 161, 570); 1261 (cf.*Ingr.* 90–186); 1306 (cf. n.14 above); 1336 (cf. *Ingr.* 99–109) etc.

38. *Ingr.* 55–60.

39. *C.Coll.*7.2 Plinval (see above, n.8) 350, calls it, generously, 'cette brillante paraphrase' of Augustine's sermon.

40. *In.Johann,Evang.Tract.* XXVI.4.

41. I wish to thank Professor E.A. Thompson for warnings of thin ice (which I have not always heeded) and much other kindness.

IV

SOZOMEN AND EUSEBIUS: THE LAWYER AS CHURCH HISTORIAN IN THE FIFTH CENTURY

Jill Harries

The legal advocate Sozomen[1] wrote his *Ecclesiastical History* in Greek in Constantinople some time in the 440s, perhaps in 443.[2] It was dedicated to the reigning Eastern Roman Emperor Theodosius II (408–450). The nine books of the *History* cover the period from the third consulship of the Caesars Crispus and Constantine (324) to the seventeenth of Theodosius II in 439. Contemporaries of Sozomen, including another lawyer Socrates Scholasticus, made attempts at the same subject and these, with others, represent a cultural flowering under Theodosius in Constantinople as yet insufficiently appreciated.

Two aspects of this renaissance deserve attention. One is the part played in it by lawyers and law. How much was Sozomen inspired by the much-heralded appearance of the Theodosian Code in 438, and how much did he make use of it? The other is an apparently conscious attempt by Sozomen, as by Socrates, to redefine ecclesiastical history, a genre dominated by its founder, Eusebius of Caesarea, as a proper subject for secular historians. These two themes are interwoven in what follows.

Both Eusebius and Sozomen were Greek men of letters. But Eusebius was also a bishop and therefore regarded doctrinal orthodoxy as being of supreme importance. Sozomen, although at pains to demonstrate his own orthodoxy, also had the literary preoccupations of his own rhetorical training and therefore accepted that heretics could also be eloquent men – and should be praised as such. Indeed, he went further: questions of dogma were matters of personal opinion which should be handled by the proper authorities — and should be excluded from the writing of history (*HE* III.15):

> on dogma, let those for whom it is right pass judgement; it is not my task to write about such things nor suitable for a history, the function of which is to treat of what is, without introducing personal opinions.

Not that Sozomen entirely avoids discussion of doctrine; in a history largely devoted to quarrels between churches this would have been hard to achieve. But his assertion of the neutrality appropriate to a historian does mark a conscious effort to define how history, including ecclesiastical history, should be written,[3] and contains an implicit challenge to the values of Eusebius.

On the subject of research, Sozomen shows an affinity not only with Eusebius but also with earlier secular Greek historians, such as Dio Cassius or Herodian,[4] whose histories were the product not only of wide reading but also of conversations with eye-witnesses of events and of personal observation. To have 'been there' at events, however trivial, was a great bonus for a historian, and Sozomen was no exception (*HE* 1.1):

> I shall mention events at which I was present or which I heard about from those who knew and saw them both in my own lifetime and before;

but for the first part of his history, Sozomen had had to travel widely, or so it seems, to collect his material:

> for earlier times I have acquired information from the laws passed about religion, and periodic synods and changes and upheavals, and from the letters of emperors and bishops, some of which are preserved to this day in the archives of the imperial palace and in churches, while others are kept scattered about in the files of learned men.

These documents Sozomen often summarised but on occasion, following the practice established by Eusebius, presented in full.

But was Sozomen as conscientious a researcher as he claimed? Parts of his *History* betray an undue fondness for a convenient literary source; the excessive coverage accorded to events in Gaul in the early fifth century (*HE* IX.11–15) deriving from Olympiodorus of Thebes unbalances the structure of the last book and has little relevance to any ecclesiastical theme. So did Sozomen always take the easy way out?

The reign of Constantine provides a good test both of Sozomen's use of sources and of his attitude to Eusebius. Before embarking on his *Ecclesiastical History*,[5] Sozomen had composed a work in two books (now lost) on church history down to the Great Persecution under Diocletian, the period covered by Eusebius' *History*. It was perhaps during his reading for the earlier work that Sozomen began to formulate his views on Eusebius' approach to ecclesiastical history, which he was to elaborate, mostly by implication, in his own larger work. For Constantine, too, Eusebius had produced the standard work, his *Life of Constantine*; one could hardly ignore it. But Sozomen was also a lawyer, and an examination of how Sozomen used both Eusebius and laws of Constantine drawn from other sources to build up his own picture of

Constantine's Christian legislation reveals a more complex method of working.

It is clear that Sozomen did use Eusebius extensively. Much of Sozomen's *HE* I, 8 and 9 does overlap with Eusebius. Sozomen's *HE* I.8 follows closely a law of Constantine quoted in full by Eusebius (*VC* II.30–7), with a slight variation in the order of provisions (although in theory Sozomen could have consulted the text of the law independently). More important are shared errors; for example Sozomen takes over Eusebius' incorrect statement that Christians were appointed to most provincial governorships. And the dominant presence of Eusebius is confirmed by the fact that in both authors an account of Constantine's law against idols, sacrifices and images is immediately followed by an episode relating to the flooding of the Nile. The versions diverge in detail with Eusebius emphasising the fact that the Nile waters (on which the fertility of Egypt depended) rose thanks to the favour of the Christian God, contrary to pagan fears (or expectations), while Sozomen discussed the transfer of the Nilometer to a Christian church.[6] The coincidence of subject establishes Sozomen's debt to Eusebius beyond doubt.

However, Eusebius was not to be followed blindly. As an advocate, Sozomen was aware, as Eusebius was not, of the role of law in history (although the Romans never evolved a discipline of legal history as such). At the end of a long chapter on Constantine's laws (*HE* I.8), Sozomen self-consciously sees fit to insert a justification of his practice by way of introduction to the next, that

> laws passed in aid of the honour and establishment of worship I must list in addition to what I have already said, because they are a part of ecclesiastical history.

Where Sozomen parted company with Eusebius was not in his inclusion of the laws but in his attitude to them. The law is seen and emphasised by the lawyer-historian as an integral part of the Christian past.

Moreover, Sozomen's concern with legal niceties could result on occasion in modifications of the Eusebian version at points where the bishop displayed an over-casual attitude to the content of laws. On Constantine's abolition of the penalties for celibacy and childlessness imposed by the Augustan *lex Papia Poppaea*, Eusebius states merely (*VC* IV.26) that the childless were punished under the old law with forfeiture of the right to benefit from wills. Sozomen, however, corrects this over-simplification: under the 'ancient law' (*HE* I.9.1), unmarried people over 25 were inferior to married people, especially in that they could not inherit, unless they were next of kin; and the childless were to lose half of what was left to them. Sozomen's expansion of the subject of the law on celibacy may be in part a reflection of Eusebius' lengthy coverage, but his aim in specifying the provisions of the Augustan law seems to have been to improve on his predecessor in the light of his own legal expertise. Once again the lawyer asserts himself against the bishop.

Sozomen also had access to Constantinian legislation, complete with headings and subscriptions, independently of Eusebius. On Crispus Caesar Sozomen commented (*HE* 1.5.2) that he, with Constantine, passed 'many laws on behalf of the Christians, as to this day can be shown from the dates at the foot of the laws and the designations of the legislators at their head.' The source is clearly the laws themselves and no literary source.

But did Sozomen derive his laws from what was now the most convenient and accessible source of law, the Theodosian Code? Or did he travel and amass his material from different archives, as his introduction claimed? It is easy enough to show that Sozomen knew of more laws than the ones preserved in the Theodosian Code as we have it. On manumission in churches, for example, Sozomen knew of three laws (*HE* I.9.6). The Theodosian Code has one, of 321, the sixth century Code of Justinian a second, of 316, which mentions yet another earlier law. The three are thus accounted for and would appear to prove that Sozomen's researches went beyond the standard law book.[7]

However, that conclusion is less certain that at first sight appears, because the Theodosian Code as we have it is incomplete. It is in theory possible that the original Code contained all three of Sozomen's laws and that it was therefore indeed Sozomen's only legal source-book. As a practising advocate he must have used it as, after 438, all earlier imperial constitutions not included in it were invalid.[8] Therefore there is a strong probability that Sozomen used the Code both as a working lawyer and as an historian.

One further avenue of approach to this question may be briefly explored. The compilers of the Theodosian Code engaged in a scissors-and-paste job on the imperial constitutions unearthed by them in order to extract from them their *ius*, or legal content, as the *ius* only was to be included in the Code. Sozomen, however, seems to have used on at least one occasion a fuller text than is preserved in the Code. A law of 318 on the rights of episcopal courts (*CT* I.27.1), promulgated by Constantine and Crispus, is cited by Sozomen in paraphrase. However, the citation also contains provisions not in the Code about the obligation of provincial governors to put the law into effect, which suggests that Sozomen had before him the full original text of the law, garnered from some imperial or episcopal archive, rather than the truncated version contained in the Code. And Sozomen, as we have already seen, knew about laws promulgated by Crispus and Constantine in favour of

Christians before 326.

To some extent, then, Sozomen's claim of independent research is justified. He used Eusebius but corrected and amplified the earlier historian on some points. He almost certainly used the Theodosian Code for the sake of convenience; but he also employed archival material missed or omitted by the compilers of the Code. The influence of his legal training and values is also apparent. But none of this explains why Sozomen the lawyer elected to write ecclesiastical history.

An important, if muted, aspect of Sozomen's *History* is its anti-pagan polemical content. The object of attack was the pagan history of Eunapius of Sardis, which was to be reworked by Zosimus. As a Greek historian, Sozomen used *exempla* from Greek history in the traditional way,[9] particularly in his lengthy dedication to Theodosius II, who was praised not only as the *pius princeps* and sum total of all the Christian virtues but also as the supreme judge of literary merit. Such *exempla* were acceptable, to Sozomen, in ecclesiastical history. But he also used Greek myth and history to refute the pagan (or 'hellene') case in history, as presented in Eunapius, and it is noticeable that he engages in this type of argumentation at precisely those points where his use of Eunapius surfaces.

Two examples are of interest. The first is the famous pagan accusation, preserved in Zosimus, who derives from Eunapius, that Constantine was converted to Christianity because, while the pagan philosopher Sopater took a high moral line, Christian bishops told Constantine that he could be purified by baptism of the murder of his son Crispus in 326 (Zos. II.29 and Soz. I.5).[10] Sozomen's retort was that Constantine and Crispus had together already passed many pro-Christian laws before 326; that Sopater was miles away at the time; and anyway Sopater would have known that Heracles had been purified of the killing of his children at Athens and so would not have advised Constantine the way he allegedly did.

The second example is the treasonable attempt in the 370s by a group of pagan 'philosophers' to discover through a form of seance the name of the successor of the emperor Valens.[11] Theodorus was the man incriminated by the emergence of the first four letters of his name from the 'table' and he was a favourite of Eunapius, who moralised (fr. 38) on his fate as a man destroyed by his own virtues. Sozomen countered this with some moralising of his own (*HE* VI.35): the will of God cannot be known by divination or human effort; philosophers should not claim to be wiser than God; these pagan philosophers also disobeyed the secular law of the Romans and in addition fell short of the example of Socrates, who chose to drink the hemlock sooner than escape when he could because of his respect for the law of Athens. Once again, Sozomen showed up Eunapius' heroes' behaviour as inconsistent not only with right religion but with the example set by their own pagan forebears. Once again, too, in the respect accorded to Roman law, we may detect the legal advocate peeping between the lines.

Finally, we should consider the cultural climate which allowed lawyer-historians like Sozomen, along with Socrates, to flourish. Various indications suggest that the late fourth and early fifth centuries saw a growing awareness of the importance of past legal authorities, namely the jurists, and, following from this, of the place of law in history, which is reflected in Sozomen's statement that law is a 'part of' ecclesiastical history (I.8.14). In the Theodosian Code, casual references to the authority of 'the jurists' occur marginally more often in the legislation of Honorius (395–423) and Arcadius (395–408) than earlier; and a second-rank jurist, Q. Cervidius Scaevola, is cited by name in a law of Arcadius of 396 (*CT* IV.4.3), showing a new depth of research into past legal authorities. Non-legal works also indicate a growing sense of the role of law in the past. The biographies of emperors known as the *Historia Augusta*, compiled by a single author in the 390s, have much to say on the legal activities of early emperors. They also accept, if indeed they do not create, a virtual dynasty of jurists extending from the time of Nerva (96–7) to that of Severus Alexander (222–35); and they whitewash Ulpian, most prolific of the Severan jurists[12]. A final small straw in the wind is a curious little pamphlet known to the Middle Ages as the *Lex Dei*, which collates paraphrased Mosaic law with the Roman law of the jurists, who are cited verbatim, although there are (or were) textual problems. While this last may be no more than a freak, the at times rather unintelligent production of some legal dogsbody on the staff (possibly) of the *vicarius* of the city of Rome, it nevertheless underlines the early fifth century belief that law was relevant to history.

Likewise historical discipline was relevant to law: both alike depended on the authority of the ancients, and it was important that that authority was accurately transmitted to posterity. In 426 the ministers of Valentinian III sent to the Senate the so-called 'Law of Citations' (*CT* I.4.3). For some, this text, with its emphasis on the authority of a select five jurists (Ulpian, Papinian, Paulus, Modestinus and Gaius), represents the nadir of Roman jurisprudence. But the text goes on to concede that other authorities cited by the Big Five were also acceptable but that their accuracy should be established by a careful collation of manuscripts. This was the language that contemporary editors of the manuscripts of Livy, Apuleius or Philostratus would have understood.

It only remained, then, for the place of lawyers in cultural life to be recognised. In 425, Theodosius II reorganised the university at Constantinople, partly to cut back a proliferation of unauthorised teachers whose classes were causing overcrowding and general chaos (*CT* XIV.9.3). In the course of this he stipulated that two professors should be appointed for the teaching of the laws and statutes, and thus gave legal scholarship, hitherto centred (though not exclusively) at Berytus (Beirut), an accepted place in the cultural life of the capital. Emeritus professors at Constantinople gained honorary rank *ex vicariis* and some may appear on the board responsible for the compilation of Theodosius' law-code. Thus men responsible for the teaching of law to students who, presumably, would ultimately practise it, were also responsible for a collection which was itself designed not for academics but as the definitive source-book of imperial constitutions for working lawyers.

   This, then, was the context in which lawyers turned to the writing of church history, at a time when ideas on legal reform and on the place of law in society and in history were being widely discussed. How far Sozomen was influenced, not simply by the text of the Code after 438 but by the frenetic atmosphere that must have existed in Constantinople legal circles during the period of its compilation in the mid-430s, is impossible to judge. Nor can we tell for certain how far Theodosius II's encouragement of lawyers led Sozomen also to appreciate Theodosius as a patron of literary work. What is certain is that Sozomen, from his reading of Eusebius and of the pagan work of Eunapius, realised that he had a contribution to make to the writing of church history as a lawyer and a layman that might help to redefine the genre in fifth-century terms. Although he relied sometimes too much and too uncritically on literary sources, his independent use of legal material, his scattered comments on what was 'suitable' for ecclesiastical history and his muted polemical approach show Sozomen as an historian both conscious of his mission and a child of his time.

NOTES

This paper owes much to the helpful criticisms and suggestions of John Matthews and Brian Warmington.

1. This is known from *HE* II.3.10–11, where S. refers to one Aquilinus 'who pleads cases in the same courts as I do'. Connections with palace officials are perhaps indicated by the story of the miraculous cure of the palace doctor Probianus (*ibid.*). See *PLRE* II Salamanes Hermeias Sozomenus 2, pp. 1023–4.
2. Inferred from his reference to a 'recent' visit of Theodosius II to Heraclea Pontica (*HE praef.* 13), which has been linked to a visit to 'Heraclea' mentioned in a law of Theodosius (*Nov. Theod.* 23) of 22 May, 443. However, as Charlotte Roueché has pointed out (forthcoming paper), the Heraclea of the novella is more likely to have been Heraclea Salbake, which is near to Aphrodisias, where the law was delivered. I am grateful to Mrs Roueché for a preview of her paper.

3. Cf. Soz. *HE* IX.10 on the sack of Rome in 410; out of the many happenings that occur at the time of a great siege, S. will record those 'appropriate' to ecclesiastical history. Socrates Scholasticus had also contributed to the debate; see Soc. *HE* V, *praef.*, a long justification of the inclusion of wars in church history.

4. Cf. Dio, *Roman History* LXXIII.18.3–4; Herodian, *History* I.1.3; Soc. HE I.1.

5. Soz. *HE* 1.1.10.

6. See Soz. *HE* I.8.5 with Eus. *VC* II.44, the appointment of Christian governors and prohibition of sacrifices aimed at pagan officials; and Eus. *VC* IV.25, prohibition of sacrifice and issue of Nile flooding.

7. *CJ* I.13.1 (316) to bishop Protogenes (of Serdica?); *CT IV.7.1* = *CJ* I.13.2 (321) to Hosius of Cordoba. These were initially individual decisions but must quickly have become general rules; see Fergus Millar, *The Emperor in the Roman World* (1977), 591. It is unlikely that S. found these in the episcopal archives of Cordoba or Serdica. He therefore saw them either as copies in the imperial archives or in the full text of the *CT*.

8. *CT* I.1.6.3 (435), '(codicis) nullumque extra se novellae constitutioni locum relicturi', with *Nov. Theod.* 1.3.

9. e.g. Cretans' honouring of Homer and other poets (*praef.* 6); Alexander and the cup of water in the Gedrosian desert (*praef.* 14); the wintering of the Argonauts at Hemona (I.6); Sibylline Oracle (II.1). Polemical use of such stories occurs at I.7 (Didyma oracle consulted by Licinius).

10. For the context, see F. Paschoud, 'Zosime 2,29 et la version paienne de la conversion de Constantin', *Historia* 20 (1971), 334–353.

11. See Zos. IV.13f. but also Amm. Marc. XXIX.1.29, who has details not in Zosimus/Eunapius. For Socrates' rather banal coverage of the same episode, see Soc. *HE* IV.19.

12. For the *HA* on jurists, see R. Syme, 'Fiction about jurists', *Zeitschrift der Savigny-Stiftung für Rechtsgeschichte (Römische Abteilung)* 97 (1980), 78–104 = *Roman Papers* III, 1393–1414.

V

HISTORY AS TEXT:
COPING WITH PROCOPIUS

Averil Cameron

An alternative title for this paper might be 'Procopius and Interpretation'. But it would be truer to talk of *mis*interpretation, for it would be fair to say that a kind of assumption still prevails that Procopius is, in the words of Bury, 'the most excellent Greek historian since Polybius'.[1] Broadly, this judgement assumes that he was critical, reliable, classical, concerned with causes... and so on. Add to that the fact that he was literally an eye-witness of quite a lot of what he describes, that he was close to Belisarius and that he took part sometimes on missions himself. He seems to have the best possible credentials.

And yet Procopius was an author trying to write classical history nearly two centuries after Ammianus. Any writer with these ambitions in sixth-century Constantinople might be expected to have encountered difficulties.

And there is a further problem, specific to Procopius; for the very same author also wrote a flattering panegyric on Justinian's buildings, and a vitriolic attack on the same emperor.[2] Doesn't this detract from the reputation of the historian, or make us wonder whether in fact the interpretations offered in the *Wars* will stand up to scrutiny? That, however, is a matter of our responses. For most admirers of the *Wars* the response has been very simple: to privilege the *Wars* and explain away the other two works by one means or another, from the most extreme — denial of Procopian authorship, to the most common — trivialisation, explaining them in terms of incidents in Procopius's biography (about which, incidentally, we know nothing outside his own works).

The *Secret History* remained unknown until after the reputation of the *Wars* was assured; consequently it is not very surprising that the Roman lawyers of the seventeenth century refused to believe that it could be by Procopius.[3] As recently as 1889, Bury still thought it spurious,[4] and it remains a problem for those who are most impressed by the supposed classicism of the *Wars*. By 1923 Bury had decided that Procopius wrote it, but thought he must have suffered a 'brainstorm' first;[5] Gibbon thought that it must 'sully the reputation and detract from the credit of Procopius'[6] — at the same time, of course, relishing its more salacious bits with prurient comment. The Penguin translator is equally embarrassed, but solves his problem by supposing that Procopius meant it as a moral tract: 'Procopius was unquestionably on the side of the right, and the things which are disgusting to us were equally disgusting to him'.[7] Jones's approach was different, but equally aimed at minimising the importance of the awkward *Secret History* : it should be disregarded, in comparison with the *Wars*, since it is merely a 'venomous pamphlet, which does not deserve the respect which is often accorded to it'.[8] Jones was more critical of the *Wars* than most, but his critique is interesting, when it complains of 'a childish credulity displayed towards everything of which the author had no personal knowledge' — as though autopsy automatically guaranteed reliability.

At least the *Secret History* has received attention, if of the wrong sort. But the *Buildings* has, if anything, suffered more seriously (even if now it is getting attention in the current boom in late Roman archaeology). It is mostly dismissed (even by Downey, who has written most on it)[9] as a sycophantic panegyric, with the implication that since the *Secret History* represents Procopius' 'true' feelings, the *Buildings* is therefore insincere. I need not underline the fact that this kind of judgement imports entirely modern assumptions about 'sincerity', and ignores the function of panegyric — which must be both one of the most central forms of expression in late antiquity, and the one least appreciated by modern scholars. I am not sure that anyone until very recently has seen more than this in the *Buildings*,[10] and there is invariably an overtone of distaste in modern references to it. If a more positive view is now emerging, it is purely because the last decade or so has seen a much more serious interest in sixth-century archaeology, and a more urgent need to look at Procopius' evidence for what it really is — in other words, it is a re-evaluation that springs from strictly utilitarian motives, not from a rereading of Procopius' work as a whole.

It seems to me, then, that although there are some signs of a new look, the interpretation of Procopius as a whole is still locked into an outmoded view of literature and thought in the sixth century, according to which a premium is placed on what is perceived as 'classical'. Procopius, in other words, is still being judged by the wrong criteria. Since he is the sole source for so much of what he tells us, and the major source for the period, it is of vital importance to understand him properly.

But even that is to assume that talking of what is 'classical' is a simple matter. Under Justinian, the concept of tradition and thus of classicism acquired a new relevance. It was not necessarily understood in the way in which we understand it now. Thus we cannot simply assume that because, for instance, Procopius writes the *Wars* in a manner reminiscent, however superficially, of Thucydides, we can make a simple equation — that he was trying to imitate Thucydides in every way, or even his nearer models, Arrian for instance. In particular, the realm of reason and the rational, which to nineteenth century scholars seemed so easily discernible from its opposite, had become by the sixth century increasingly problematic. How then to tackle classicising history, that is by definition rational, even 'scientific', in an age of faith — unreason? We shall find that the rational Procopius, in company with most late antique writers, scientific historians or not,[11] allows in — and *has* to allow in — a very large dose of unreason, miracle, faith or whatever you like to call it, and that he does so without forfeiting the right to claim that he was writing classicising history. To judge the *Wars* and Procopius's other works by a rigid standard of what is classical (the usual procedure) is to get things the wrong way round; it is the concept of what is classical that needs to be redefined.

A very brief comment about Justinianic art might be useful at this point, since this judgement of Procopius often hangs together with a view of the reign in terms of an encouragement of classical learning and a revival of classicising art. But classical revivals — at least when defined as such by modern scholars — are now suspect. The most lively recent evaluation of Justinian[12] sees him not as the champion of a wishy-washy kind of Christian Hellenism, but in the guise of Stalin, with purges and exile, the Byzantine equivalent of labour-camps. Cyril Mango, incidentally, prefers the analogy of Nazi Germany.[13] The 'classical' Procopius, like the classical revival in Justinianic art, belongs to a particular aspect of the period, and was emphasised at a particular stage in modern scholarship; but it never told the whole story, and certainly cannot do so now. It was Justinian who burnt books, arrested intellectuals, closed the Academy and ended the consulship, as it was Justinian's troops who rode down the people in the Hippodrome; and when Procopius wrote in the preface to the *Secret History* that publication could mean death for himself and his family he knew what he was talking about. If the *Wars* gives us a comfortingly classical impression, that is our problem.

Procopius' works have so far always been interpreted by reference to the author. We should start rather from the texts themselves.

How then to tackle the problem? The first way would be to show that the three are not contradictory at all, except in the superficial and obvious sense. They are all, if you like, elitist works, all using the same high style and purist Greek, even to the extent of carrying through a strict and idiosyncratic prose rhythm; the *Secret History* is not a subversive work in the sense either that it might reach a different audience or that it used different categories of thought and language from the other, public, works. Each one is in linguistic terms as artificial as the other;[14] none, therefore, can be presumed to be a straightforward expression of Procopius' 'real' views. Each one has a rhetorical preface distinct from the rest of the work, made up of a mingling of stock themes from authors such as Diodorus, and this is as true, again, of the 'secret' *Secret History* as it is of the public works. Stylistic analysis would show no significant difference between the three. And they share a unity of phraseology and ideas, the same categories of thought. Between the *Secret History* and *Wars*, further, there is a constant cross-referencing and self-allusion; the *Secret History* also seems to point forward to the *Buildings*, and refers to plans for a different type of work in which ecclesiastical matters would be fully covered. To some extent, then, Procopius himself seems to have seen his works as a whole, and we are certainly justified in trying to take them as a system instead of as the direct expressions of Procopius's state of mind at any given time.

A naively biographical approach, then, is not adequate. Furthermore, the relative chronology of the three works is not finally settled. Whereas of the eight books of the *Wars*, it is clear that I–VII were finished and published in 551, while book VIII was added three years or so later, the matter is not so clear in the case of the *Secret History* or the *Buildings*. The former, in my view, was begun simultaneously with *Wars* VII, and left unfinished in 550; it is still however sometimes dated to *c.* 560. As for the *Buildings*, opinions differ between 554 and *c.* 560 and there is not enough clear evidence to settle the matter either way. My preferences are for the earlier dates in both cases.[15] Thus the three texts belong closely together. If the *Secret History* and the *Buildings* belonged to *c.* 560, the supposed problem of contradiction would be as serious, while if the *Secret History* belonged to 550 and the *Buildings* ten years later, we should still have to try to reconcile the *Secret History* and the *Wars*. A far better approach is to abandon these speculations for the time being and look to see what actual similarities there might be in the works. For what it is worth, I place no faith in the dubious suggestion that our Procopius was prefect of the city in 562,[16] and think it very likely that he died soon after 554. Thus the texts themselves constitute our only data; there is no external evidence to help us.

I want therefore to suggest some ways in which the three texts hang together and share a common set of ideas as well as a common linguistic texture. The *Wars*, usually thought so self-evidently superior to the other works, will turn out in fact to be very similar to them.

First, miracle. The books normally assume that it is easy to isolate Procopius' religious views. Thus he is conventionally regarded as a sceptic unusual for his age. But this is to take at face value passages better explained, in my view, by the difficulty which Procopius found in accommodating Christianity in his secular history. In fact it is very easy to find examples of the miraculous, even in the *Wars*, ranging from the curiosity or prodigy to the full-scale scenario. I shall restrict myself to a small selection. Thus, to set against those passages where he professes ignorance of Christianity as though it is some barbarian curiosity, there are those where he tells without sign of disbelief how St Peter protected the walls of Rome,[17] how the mosaic of Theoderic disintegrated and foretold the future,[18] how Belisarius' wine jars miraculously overflowed,[19] how when some Romans tried to open the doors of the temple of Janus, they would not move, showing how wrong it was to think of returning to pagan practice.[20]

Much more significant than these portents and isolated incidents — like the two-headed child born at Edessa, for instance[21] — are the cases where Procopius has shaped his narrative at a focal point around a miraculous story. Take for example the dispatch of the Vandal expedition, one of the most carefully presented sections of the *Wars*, and the most dramatic; according to Procopius, no-one supported Justinian's idea of an expedition against the Vandals until one of the priests they call bishops (a nice contradictory touch) told the emperor that he had had a dream in which God had told him to rebuke Justinian for hesitation when God was on his side.[22] Procopius develops further the theme of divine aid for the expedition, even to the extent of placing himself in the narrative: he himself had been among the doubters, he says, until he too had had a prophetic dream.[23] As we know, the expedition enjoyed an amazing success, and Belisarius' entry to Carthage is endowed by Procopius with miraculous qualities; not only did he himself earn greater fame than any of his predecessors or contemporaries, but the invading army behaved in the most remarkable way, with no looting or any kind of disturbance whatsoever. And this was confirmation of a dream experienced by many Roman Africans, Procopius says, who had seemed to see the figure of S. Cyprian telling them that he would avenge the loss of his church[24] – the great basilica outside the walls of Carthage overlooking the sea, which had fallen into Arian hands during the Vandal rule.

We must stay with this passage a little longer, for now Procopius develops the theme even more fully: the Arian clergy, who had been preparing for the saint's feastday, cleaning and hanging up the lamps and church treasures, ran away in confusion when the Byzantines entered the city, so that the Catholics (in Procopius' terminology 'the Christians who practise the orthodox faith') were able to walk into the basilica and celebrate the saint's day with the church decorations that the Arians had prepared, just as Belisarius and Procopius had entered the palace of the Vandal king, and eaten the food and wine prepared for him.

This is one of the high peaks of the supposedly 'sceptical' *Wars*, yet

Procopius chooses most deliberately to begin and end his account of this greatest of Belisarius' victorious campaigns with a Christian miracle that is fulfilled. It is only one of the most notable of many similar appearances of miracle in the *Wars*. Often, as here, told in the language of 'objectivity', but miracle for all that.

If these instances are to be taken seriously, as I suggest, then they do not cohere well with the causal rationale of history assumed by modern scholars on the basis of the historiographical style of the *Wars*.[25] But in practice, we look in vain to the *Wars* for an analysis of 'true' and underlying 'causes' in the Thucydidean or Polybian manner. Instead, there seem to be two ways in which Procopius can explain events — by reference either to character and personality (I shall return to this later) or to divine intervention. He feels that some discussion of causes is incumbent on him, but whenever he attempts it, we find him falling back on the notion that all is in fact directed by God, even if we cannot see why. Thus the miracles instanced above represent for Procopius a sufficient and a satisfactory historical explanation. Let us take a famous passage as an example — the description of the terrible sack of Antioch by Chosroes in 540, sometimes quite wrongly taken to imply scepticism. Before the event, there was a portent: the standards of the troops turned round of their own accord. But the meaning of this was naturally only evident after the event, of which Procopius writes: 'when I write about such a great disaster and pass it on to posterity, my head spins and I cannot understand why God should want to raise up an individual or a place and then cast him down and extinguish him for no apparent reason'. He concludes, however, that we must hold on to the belief that all is for the best, all part of God's inscrutable plan, and it is for him merely an added element of the incomprehensible, not material for doubt, that Antioch, the 'city of God', should have been sacked by a man 'of the utmost impiety', and that one of the few buildings left standing was a Christian church.[26] Other passages in the *Wars* convey the same sense that for Procopius, history was the result of God's direct intervention. At the decisive battle of Ad Decimum in the *Vandal War*, he remarks on what he describes as God's way of manipulating events to the desired conclusion, how He influences men's minds to choose the wrong course[27] and in a memorable passage in the *Gothic Wars* he gives it as his opinion that God had decided that Totila should prosper — hence whatever Belisarius did, he was bound to be thwarted by fortune.[28] It does not much matter whether he writes in terms of fortune, or God, or both, since the notion is the same — some superhuman agency is deciding affairs outside the control of men. Such reasoning is incompatible with the search for human causes, and sure enough, we do not actually find much of the latter in the *Wars*.

On the human scale, Procopius tends to seek explanations in terms of character, especially those of the rulers or their representatives. The personality of Chosroes is given great prominence in the *Persian Wars*; campaigns begin and end because of it, and the whole set of Persian incursions in book II is presented in terms of a game of cat and mouse between Chosroes and the towns of the eastern borders. And here is a feature that links the *Wars* with both the *Secret History* and the *Buildings* — the centrality of the individual and specifically of the emperor. For Procopius, as all three works demonstrate, the course of contemporary history must — indeed can only — be explained in terms of the personality of the emperor.

We can now see how the most awkward aspects of the *Secret History* — its demonology — and of the *Buildings* — its panegyrical treatment — are in Procopius' terms entirely explicable and coherent. For the demonology of the *Secret History*, regarded by many as satire, or a bad joke unworthy of Procopius, is demanded by the dilemma in which the historian now found himself: if the personality of the ruler is at the heart of political explanation, and if God directs events, how to explain a bad ruler who in Procopius's eyes has caused disaster otherwise than by linking him with the devil? Procopius lived in a world where demons were always round the corner and could hardly be kept at bay; it was an easy step to attribute the bad results he now saw in Justinian's rule to demons, and a necessary one to link them with the personalities of the emperor and empress, who are, in a memorable passage, said themselves to be a pair of demons.[29] It was also an easy way out — neither God himself nor the empire as such were to blame, only Justinian himself. And this leads into the question of the *Buildings* : how could Procopius possibly represent the same emperor there as inspired by God and as the embodiment of the ideal of the Christian empire? For that is what he does. He represents Justinian as having a hot-line to God, a special relation whereby he could initiate on earth the divine plans vouchsafed to him, which is, of course, the standard late antique political philosophy reiterated by several writers in Procopius' own day. Of course, there *is* a prima facie contradiction between this and the *Secret History*, and we cannot know what specific reason caused Procopius to write the *Buildings* — perhaps simply an imperial commission. But the *Buildings*, by placing the emperor at the centre, and by attributing results on earth to the combination of imperial action and supernatural direction, works within the same general framework as the *Wars* and the *Secret History*; supposing that we are interested in what Procopius 'really' thought, and supposing that to be possible, there is no reason to imagine that he did not hold to the overall conception expressed in the *Buildings* of human personality being directed from outside by the divine. It is merely the inverse of the explanation of the *Secret History* — the explanation of the good instead of the explanation of the bad; the type of explanation itself remains the same. Neither of these works (and not the *Wars* either, as we shall see) tells the whole of what Procopius wants to say about Justinian; one is not more 'true' than the other, or more representative of his 'real' views.

I want to go on to expand further on this idea, and explain why these three types of work should all have been necessary and why they must be read on equal terms. But first I shall put forward some of the categories within which all three operate, and which are both limiting factors in relation to options open to a writer in the period and contributory to the unity of the three works.

Any reader of Procopius is struck at once by the sharp — not to say schematised — views which he expresses about human affairs and human nature. The rhetoric of all three works is a class rhetoric; the author comes forward as the spokesman of the wealthy classes protesting against the change represented by an innovating emperor. It is a matter of simple polarities. All three texts work with an elaborate set of exclusions. Judgements are made in all three works according to the extent to which these demarcation lines are observed.

Barbarians, women and the lower classes ('rabble' or 'trouble-makers') come first to mind. The last two are the simpler — the lower classes are prone to folly and mischief, unlike the well-to-do; they are responsible, according to the *Buildings*, for the Nika revolt.[30] Women are to be viewed with suspicion; it is deplorable and surprising that some of them followed the factions, and it is supposed that women in general are only interested in male physique — as the Gothic women marvel at the physical superiority of the invading Byzantines over their own men.[31] Theodora herself represents the undue prominence of women; under her influence *all* women are said to have become depraved.[32] The characterisation of Belisarius' wife, Antonina, whom Procopius knew very well and had accompanied on various missions, owes a great deal to this rhetoric; she was remarkable *for a woman*[33] (so too was the Gothic queen Amalasuntha).[34] Undoubtedly he builds up Antonina as a foil for Theodora; both, as powerful women, play a functional role in the structure and thought of the *Secret History*, where one of his chief taunts against Belisarius is precisely that he was too much in thrall to a woman — Antonina.[35] The times are out of joint: a woman saves the day in the Nika revolt, with a self-conscious speech about role reversal.[36]

As for barbarians, they are presumed to be both treacherous and foolishly simple, sometimes useful as buffers against a greater evil but naturally inferior. Room can be made within this view for admiration for barbarian royalty (Theodoric), especially for nobility in defeat

(Gelimer).[37] The Persian Chosroes occupies a special position as counterbalance to Justinian, and much play is made on the theme of his 'barbarian character'.[38] It is axiomatic that civilisation should be brought to these barbarians — which meant Byzantine rule, or Byzantine conversion. In the *Buildings*, the very building works themselves in the provinces evince the theory — they are either defensive and military or churches built as outposts of Byzantine orthodoxy and with the intention of converting and impressing the natives: conversion went hand in hand with reconquest, and was as much taken for granted.

In the *Secret History*, Justinian may be criticised for his wars, on the grounds of the thousands killed, the way that Africa was left a desert, in Procopius' phrase;[39] but this is part of the attack on Justinian himself, an example of the heuristic emphasis on imperial character. It does not imply that the war policy itself was wrong, but rather that it was not carried out well in practice. Its ultimate failure was thus a token of Justinian's nature. As the *Wars* progressed, Procopius did have some difficulty with his over-simple idea of barbarians, and in book VIII there is a new and deliberate sympathy for the Gothic cause under the leadership of Totila. For a short time, the roles assigned to barbarians and Romans by Procopius were reversed. But by and large the opposition 'barbarian/civilised' holds good. Correspondingly, whole sections of Byzantine society can be dismissed as 'wicked', while those who are praised are praised in restricted and undifferentiated vocabulary. People of all ranks of society are assumed to act from simple motives (often from greed), and such motives are presented as though they are adequate explanatory devices.

The opposition 'order/disorder' is very strong in these texts as an explanatory device. A chief criticism of Justinian is that he is constantly 'stirring things up' — by implication unnecessarily; that he creates disorder where order had prevailed. He represents the topsy-turvy; he dresses wrongly, acts unexpectedly and generally makes the government look like a children's game, or like something on the stage.[40] The Nika revolt, therefore, is explained in the *Wars* by the zeal of the factions for 'disorder'; the Blues and Greens are perceived as wanting trouble for its own sake. It is emphasised that they have 'no reason'.[41] Chosroes has a similar character to Justinian's, in Procopius' analysis, and the same vocabulary of disorder is used of him; seen from the other point of view, Procopius could only explain the war between Persia and Byzantium in terms of a clash between two personalities, both wantonly seeking trouble. Like the Nika revolt, the plague signifies the ultimate disorder.[42] Nothing is expected in its course, not even according to the accepted canons of epidemics. And the accounts of these two disasters have been carefully and explicitly structured so as to present an analogy with corresponding misfortunes experienced by Chosroes — reversals in each case following on a monarch who does not conform to the expectation. Not only is Chosroes not like an ordinary king; he is characterised by *apanthropia*, he is not even like a normal human being.[43] If personality is the key to historical explanation, disaster must be related to a disordered personality at the centre of things. Perpetual activity, marked outwardly by extreme asceticism, displays Justinian no less than Chosroes at the heart of events.

The *Buildings* shows the operation of the same categories, but in reverse. From being the creator of disorder, Justinian is here presented as its restorer; he rescued the state when it was 'tottering', he brought harmony and internal peace, codified the laws which were 'murky and in confusion', restored the faith, which was 'wandering', to its true path, built cities and strengthened frontiers.[44] This is an ideal. To what extent Procopius assented to all of these propositions does not matter for my purpose; what does matter is that he is using the same vocabulary of order and disorder in all his works — and does not go beyond it. Underlying the *Buildings* is a theory familiar from many expositions of imperial political theory since Eusebius — that of an ordered universe in which the emperor directed earthly business in calm imitation of the heavenly macrocosm. His function, therefore, is to bring order. If he is to be criticised, it will be for bringing *dis*order, and those who are to be blamed in society are those who 'stir up trouble'. There is no space in this view for change and development — and no need. The emperor, then, is specially close to God in a unique way, and must be personally responsible, with God's aid, for what happens in his kingdom. Conversely, if things go wrong, the relation between God and the emperor must have been broken — as we see in the *Secret History*. Furthermore, these three texts share in a discourse common to other contemporary writings.

There is a good deal, for instance (only to take one example) in the closely contemporary work of John the Lydian about the special role of the emperor as restorer of things that had gone wrong.[45] But the dominance of the 'classicising' interpretation of Procopius has prevented scholars from recognising how strongly the same discourse is present in Procopius. He was not the uniquely rational and objective historian usually assumed, but part of, and equally shaped by, the discourse of his time.

So it is helpful, I suggest, to look at the *Buildings* less as a personal document about Justinian, the very same emperor so vilified in the *Secret History*, than as a de-personalised statement of the ideal relations between emperor, God and empire. It then becomes much easier to recognise that it draws on the same vocabulary of oppositions, the same basic assumptions, as the *Wars* and *Secret History*. The three works differ in kind — the *Buildings* is more static, much less time-bound than the other two, synchronic rather than diachronic. But they share a unified rhetoric and a unified system of ideas.

I have only been able to set out this unity in a cursory way. I should like to move briefly on to the question 'why?'. *Why* did Procopius write in the way he did, in three works that are superficially so much at odds, instead of in a unified history that would do justice to all his ideas — for the *Wars*, for all its voluminousness, almost seems to leave out Justinian altogether? There must be more to it, surely, than the mere accidentals of Procopius' own biography.

In the first place, a great change had taken place during the writing of the *Wars*, as happened to Eusebius during the writing of the *Church History*. Procopius was overtaken by events: the story of victory became a story of tedious difficulty and delay. But I want to stress two other explanations: they are parallels, not alternatives.

The first is a simple one — writers were not free under Justinian to write as they felt.[46] Even if Procopius had been capable of a full explanation of the wars which *would* take into account the failings of Byzantine policy and practice, he could hardly have published it just like that. As it is, the *Wars* began as a grand and patriotic record, but turned into something more complex — and then Procopius found himself in difficulties. The *Secret History* was the safety valve for all that could not be said in the *Wars*, a history composed in a political and cultural climate when panegyric was the order of the day. A truly critical secular history was hardly possible in this society, either in personal terms for its author (for lawyers, teachers and intellectuals were targets of actual persecution) or in terms of finding a workable mode of historical explanation. Procopius needed the *Buildings* and the *Secret History* to present his whole picture of Justinian, for it could not be done otherwise. I do not, of course, mean to imply that presenting a rounded picture of Justinian was ever Procopius' intention; rather that the three separate works do in practice do that in terms of the categories used.

We might however look also for a structural explanation. The three works are as they are because of the society which produced them. In the lifetime of Procopius there was no cultural synthesis but on the contrary an extreme polarity. The civic structure of the Late Empire survived pretty well in the east, until the plagues of 542, with a mortality perhaps approaching 50 per cent, did more than anything else to cut it off, as it did also to undermine the reality of reconquest. Within the cities, some practised classical types of literary expression at the highest technical levels, while others, like the deacon and poet Romanos, made a cult of feigned ignorance. Paul the Silentiary, one of the best erotic poets for centuries, also wrote elaborate Christian panegyric. Even if the Academy at Athens in some sense continued after 529,[47] which I doubt, it did so only in the wings, and overshadowed by a culture which placed more emphasis on public theological debates than on philosophy. The reigning emperor advertised himself as the restorer of the empire while conducting savage purges of dissidents. It was not surprising that the young followers of the Blues and Greens resorted to violence in a society that was so polarised, and where the educated classes, of which Procopius was a member, could no longer be sure that they had the entrée to office. The pattern of thought represented in the *Wars*, the *Secret History* and the *Buildings* is fragmented, like the cultural background from which it came. The binary oppositions which are so striking a feature of all three texts reflect the oppositions in contemporary society. The ultimate opposition is the superficial opposition between the three works themselves, yet this too is subverted by their underlying unity.

A list of omissions in Procopius' work would be long. He did not give a whole picture — never mentioning for instance, the great Ecumenical Council of 553 or the decade of polemic that preceded it, or the ferment of easterners and westerners in Constantinople, come to take one side or the other, who all too often ended up in prison or in exile. For if the three texts share a common texture, nevertheless each, but especially the *Wars*, was also regulated by a stylised classicising vocabulary and form. It was literally impossible for the *Wars* to accommodate a wider range of relevant contemporary material. The *Secret History* and the *Buildings* were natural and necessary extensions.

Procopius the historian will elude us so long as we continue to suppose that his writings are a simple key to his personal history. The texts are not so easily read. So why not change our focus from the historian to the texts? The immediate result would be a retreat from the assumption that the *Wars* is 'better' than the other two, and hence automatically more reliable. And that is the first step towards a less superfical characterisation of the 'classicism' of the age of Justinian.

NOTES

1. J.B. Bury, *History of the Later Roman Empire*, 2nd ed. (London, 1923), II, 419; endorsed by E. Stein, *Histoire du Bas-Empire* II (Amsterdam, 1949), 710.
2. See Averil Cameron, *Procopius and the Sixth Century* (London, 1985); J.A.S. Evans, *Procopius* (New York, 1971); B. Rubin, *Prokopios von Kaisareia* (Stuttgart, 1954 = PW, vol. 23.1, cols. 273–599, 1957).
3. On the rediscovery of the *Secret History*, see S. Mazzarino, *The End of the Ancient World* (Eng. trans., London, 1966), 102 ff.

4. J. B. Bury, *History of the Later Roman Empire (395 A.D. to 800)* (London, 1889), I, 359 ff, cf. 364 'It is almost impossible to believe that Procopius ... would have ever used the exaggerated language in which the author of the *Secret History* pours out the vials of his wrath upon Justinian'.

5. *op. cit.* (n. 1), 421 f. Nevertheless, this discussion (in Bury's second edition) remains in many ways the clearest and most helpful introduction to Procopius's work.

6. *Decline and Fall*, IV, chap. 20.

7. G.A. Williamson, *Procopius, The Secret History* (Harmondsworth, 1966), 31.

8. A.H.M. Jones, *The Later Roman Empire: a Social and Economic Survey* (Oxford, 1964), I, 266.

9. See e.g. G. Downey, 'The Composition of Procopius, *De Aedificiis*', TAPA 78 (1947), 171–83, with 'Procopius on Antioch: a study of method in the *De Aedificiis*', *Byzantion* 14 (1939), 361–78; 'The Persian Campaign in Syria in A.D. 540', *Speculum* 28 (1953), 340–48; 'Notes on Procopius, *De Aedificiis* Book I', *Studies presented to D.M. Robinson*, II (St. Louis, 1953), 719 ff.

10. Now see B. Croke and J. Crow, 'Procopius on Dara', *JRS* 73 (1983), 143–59, with Cameron, *op. cit.* (n.2), chap. 6.

11. Some interesting remarks are to be found in E. Gabba, 'True History and False History in Classical Antiquity', *JRS* 71 (1981), 50–62. On imitation of the classics by historians like Procopius see K. Adshead, 'Thucydides and Agathias', in B. Croke and A. Emmett, *History and Historians in Late Antiquity* (Sydney, 1983), 82–87.

12. Tony Honoré, *Tribonian* (London, 1978), chap. 1; Justinianic classicism: e.g. E. Kitzinger, *Byzantine Art in the Making* (Cambridge, Mass., 1977), 98.

13. C. Mango, *Byzantium. The Empire of New Rome* (London, 1981), 135.

14. The stylistic unity of the three works (and thus the Procopian authorship of the *Secret History*) was established by J. Haury, *Procopiana* (Augsburg, 1891) and 'Zu Prokops Geheimgeschichte', *Byz. Zeit.* 34 (1934), 10–14.

15. See Cameron, *op. cit.* (n.2), chap. 1; but Evans, *op. cit.* (n.2), supports the later dates, and L.M. Whitby argues again for the later date for the *Buildings* in *JHS* (1985) 129–47.

16. Based on the *Chronicle* of John of Nikiu, trans. Charles, p. 92.

17. *BG* I.23. 4 f. Apparent ignorance of Christian terms: e.g. *BP* I.18.15, 25.32; II.26.2 etc. But this is only part of a general stylistic trait: cf. the list in my *Agathias* (Oxford, 1970), App. J.

18. *BG* I.24.22 f.

19. *BG* III.35.4 f.

20. *BG* I.25.18 f.

21. *BG* IV.14.39 f.

22. *BV* I.10.1 f., 18.

23. I.12.3.

24. I.21.6, 17 f.

25. But for the appearance of such features in other secular histories, see L. Cracco Ruggini, 'The Ecclesiastical Histories and the Pagan Historiography: Providence and Miracles', *Athenaeum* n.s. 55 (1977), 107–26.

26 *BP* II.10. See Averil Cameron, 'The "Scepticism" of Procopius', *Historia* 15 (1966), 6–25.

27. *BV* I.19.25.

28. *BG* III.13.15 f.

29. *Secret History* 12; 30.34. On the centrality of emperors see also L. Cracco Ruggini, 'Imperatori e uomini divini (I–VI secolo)', *Passato presente* 2: *Governanti e*

intellettuali; popolo di Roma e popolo di Dio, ed. P. Brown, L. Cracco Ruggini, M. Mazza (Turin, 1982), 9–91, especially 26; 'Potere e carismi in età imperiale', *Studi storici* 3 (1979), 585–607.

30. *Buildings* I.I.20.
31. *BP* I.24.6 (the whole passage — again on the Nika revolt — is orchestrated in terms of disorder, represented by women, the Blues and Greens and the common people); *BG* II.29.34.
32. See especially *Secret History* 17.24 f.: injured husbands had to keep their mouths shut because their wives would go straight to the empress and then the husbands would be punished.
33. See e.g. *B.G.* II.4.20. On Procopius' treatment of Theodora and Antonina, see E. Fisher, 'Theodora and Antonina in the *Historia Arcana*: History and/or Fiction?', *Arethusa* 11 (1978), 253–79.
34. *BG* I.2.21.
35. Belisarius: see especially *Secret History*, chaps. 1–5; cf. 4.22 (his terror at facing the empress after she and Antonina had turned against him):
    'There was no honourable thought in his head; he was not conscious that he had once been a man. The sweat ran down his face unceasingly; his head swam; his whole body trembled in an agony of despair, tormented as he was by slavish fears and anxieties utterly unworthy of a man.'
36. *BP* I.24.33 f. (presented as a curiosity, despite the tendency in modern books to take it completely at face value).
37. Barbarians: see Cameron, *op. cit.* (n.2), chap. 13. It is not only in ethnographical digressions that this attitude comes through. Procopius's admiration for Theodoric: *BG* I.1.27–28; the nobility of Gelimer: *BV* II.7.1 f.; 9.11 (compare 8.1 f., 10 for Procopius' normal attitudes to barbarians); similarly on the Goth Totila: *BG* III.2.7.
38. Chosroes: *BP* II.9.8 (similar language used of Gelimer, *BV* I.9.7); II.11.26; *Secret History* 18.26.
39. *Secret History* 18.1–9.
40. Justinian: *Secret History* 14.5, 15; 15.24 f.; his reign was marked by natural disasters (disorder in the physical world): 18.45, cf. 31 f., 37.
41. *BP* I.24.1 f., 6.
42. Plague: *BP* II.22 f.; see especially 23.12 f., 14, 17 f. and cf. *Secret History* 18.44 (plague as one of the natural disasters indicating that times were out of joint).
43. *BG* IV.10.8, with the whole narrative of the Persian wars (e.g. *BP* I.23. 1 f.).
44. *Buildings* I.1. Whereas the *Secret History* claims that Justinian's rule is like a game (n.39), here it is the great Cyrus, type of wise kingship, whose rule is made to look like a game by comparison with Justinian's: I.1.15.
45. In the *De Magistratibus*, passim. T.F. Carney, *Bureaucracy in Traditional Society: Romano-Byzantine Bureaucracies viewed from within* (Lawrence, Kansas, 1971), II, 164 f., has some interesting tables of similarities in ideas and vocabulary between John and Procopius.
46. Honoré and Mango (nn. 12 and 13) have recently laid stress on this aspect of the reign.
47. See recently H. Blumenthal, '529 and after: what happened to the Academy?', *Byzantion* 48 (1978), 369–85.

VI

THE TRIUMPH OF GRECO-ROMAN RHETORICAL ASSUMPTIONS IN PRE-CAROLINGIAN HISTORIOGRAPHY

Roger Ray

In Galatians 2:11–14, Paul recounts how once, at Antioch, he rebuked Peter for having compromised with the circumcision party. The Neoplatonist Porphyry was perhaps the most important of the pagan critics who took this little narrative as evidence that the leaders of the Early Church were at odds on central issues. Jerome, replying to Porphyry, argued that the scene at Antioch did not literally take place: it was Paul's rhetorical artifice, created out of the honorable desire to find every occasion on which to expound the doctrine of grace.[1] This exegesis touched off a long quarrel with Augustine. In the early going he complained that the admission into the biblical *historia* of even one patch of tactically falsified events will call into question the veracity of the whole narrative. If, said Augustine, the confrontation at Antioch did not occur, then in Galatians 2 Paul wrote what was false. 'And if he wrote what was false *there*, where did he write what was true?'[2]

This debate is well known, though not for the reason I mention it. It is, I believe, a revealing moment in the history of rhetorical historiography. On one thing Jerome and Augustine were agreed: Galatians 2:11–14 is historical writing. They parted ways over the substance of Paul's narrative. For Augustine it consisted of real events; for Jerome, imaginary but plausible events. Both views fall easily within the longstanding Greco-Roman assumption that history is a major form of rhetorical exposition.[3] Jerome's exegesis is a bright reflector of the utilitarianism which suffused the secondary education. In all forms of rhetorical discourse, among which history was admired almost as much as oratory, the final measure of excellence was persuasive success. It was taken for granted that the historian's ideal is to tell the truth; at the same time it was generally thought that the great value of his genre lies in its power to move people. Hence the orator and the historian had common cause, to find the available means of persuasion; and this was mainly a question of contents, not style. In the schools the rhetors taught the only well articulated method of discovery, that of *inventio*, 'the devising of contents, either true or verisimilar, which make the case seem plausible'.[4] The forensic orator and the historian even shared an interest in the narrator's art, since both sought to convince the audience to accept their preferred reading of the events in question. In fact the rhetors teach that the courtroom *narratio* stands on the same foundations as that of the historian; this comes out with special emphasis in Marius Victorinus, one of Jerome's contemporaries.[5] The inventional theory requires that one begin, as a rule, with the facts at hand, an event or set of events. Yet if witnesses, documents, and other sources of these 'inartificial' contents do not fully suffice, then the theory calls for 'art', the imaginative creation of verisimilar materials which build up the *données* into a winning larger structure. It was a method of obvious potential for historians, since it freed them from the limitations of 'inartificial' resources.[6] But there was a further possibility: Quintilian tells the forensic narrator that he should generate an entirely fictitious *narratio* if the actual facts do not tell for his case. This sort of narrative he calls *color*, not *mendacium*; it is benign rhetorical strategy, not culpable falsification.[7] It is this ambit of sharply utilitarian rhetorical thought which lies behind Jerome's exegesis of Galatians 2.

In Paul's narrative Jerome saw a well-meaning *color*, a fictious narrative written for didactic effect. In an attempt to browbeat, *more suo*, any pagan critic who might now complain that the Apostles were also liars, Jerome appeals to the routine practices and attitudes of the rhetorical schools. In the classroom declamations, he observes, fictions are common, but no one takes them for simple lying. Hence none should think that his exegesis of Galatians 2 imputes mendacity to Paul; for if youths in school may use the recognized discretionary tactics, how much more a prince of the Church.[8] Peter Wiseman has recently argued that the method of *inventio* enabled Late Republican authors like Valerius Antias to write the history of early Rome from very little evidence.[9] Jerome, a Late Roman master of Latin and Greek literature, was prepared to see this same method at work in a most admired, even saintly, historian. What did he take for granted about the practices of the rest? Certainly there was, to his mind, no necessary conflict between truthful history and rhetorical *inventio*.

Quintilian once observed that historical narrative 'gathers strength the truer it gets'.[10] This was written in respect of the ideal of truth, but surely not to suggest that history books worthy of the name contain nothing but the truth. The remark probably recognises that historical narratives are, as a rule, more or less true to fact, a composite of real and verisimilar contents in proportional relationships determined, on the one hand, by the extent and quality of the historian's sources and, on the other, by the clarity and importance of his persuasive purpose. In extra-biblical historical works this mixture would have given Augustine, the former rhetor, no pause. But when it came to the biblical *historia*, it was a different matter. Here was a book of history which bore an unprecedented burden of proof: if it is not unvaryingly true, if Jesus and the Apostles did not do and say what is recorded of them, then the Gospel collapses. Hence in the Bible Augustine saw history written with an unremitting veracity denied to all other historical narratives.[11] There was no way to account for this uniqueness except by an appeal to divine inspiration. Greco-Roman historiographical theory would not do. Nor could a disciple of Thucydides have denied it. Thucydides was a rigorous champion of truth, but even he allowed that a fine historical work combines the real and the verisimilar insofar as the author composes likely speeches for his main actors.[12] Augustine granted only the most restrained use of rhetorical verisimilitude to the sacred narrators. It was imperative to the faith, for example, that the Sermon on the Mount be very near to the *ipsissima verba domini*. Augustine did find many analogies between the methods of the Evangelists and those of classical historians, but in his view the final guarantee of the truth of *sacra historia* was, like revelation itself, miraculous.[13] Augustine took Jerome to task because in the exegesis of Galatians 2 he had written as if the Bible were just another book of history, a didactic fusion of the real and the verisimilar. To Augustine's mind divine inspiration set the Scriptural history apart from the general run.

The belief that the Bible is the perfect example of truthful narrative might have set new standards among ecclesiastical historians, but this possibility seems not to have come fully home to a Christian writer before modern times. In the early seventh century, Isidore of Seville had a brush with it. Defining the forms of narrative, he wrote that history is unlike fable because it sticks entirely to real events.[14] None of the ancients, he remarkably explains, wrote history except from their own personal experience. 'For things that are seen are published without lying.' A few lines earlier he had considered the meaning of the Greek word *historein*, to know from ocular testimony. It makes the subsequent emphasis on autopsy seem all very classical. Fontaine believes, however, that Isidore's truly formative authority was the Fourth Gospel, where (19:35) it is affirmed that the eyewitness is the guarantor of truth.[15] Thus the biblical ideal of *res verae*, not to mention poor information about the pagan *veteres*, seems to have caused Isidore to take an idiosyncratic position which is more Thucydidean than Thucydides. It was an idea without a future, especially since the task of writing history would more and more fall to authors shut away by monastic vows from the sights and sounds of the larger world. It was of little use even to Isidore; in his own historical writings autopsy was not the method, nor could he have been personally sure that *res verae* were his materials. I say this not to his discredit, but to point out that in the Early Middle Ages the most stringent theory of historical truth, stated even on the powerful biblical standard, faced stiff odds in the actual practice of the craft. Greco-Roman rhetorical assumptions had triumphed again.

Many would grant that this was true by the Carolingian period, when there was a revival of the formal study of classical rhetoric. I am convinced that the issue was never really in doubt from the beginnings of Christian historiography onwards. It is the many hagiographers and the few expansive historians who persuade me, writers who took thought to impose their will on readers and listeners. Nor do I wish to tarnish the classical credentials of Einhard. Yet he was surely not Europe's first great rhetorical historian. That title belongs, with many others, to the Venerable Bede, to whom I shall come in a moment.

First, however, some general observations about rhetoric and rhetorical assumptions. One often reads that in the Early Middle Ages rhetoric was scarcely different from grammar; it is supposed to have consisted of figures of speech, *imitatio*, clichés — in a word, style. Though I do not entirely dispute this view, I intend to use the word 'rhetoric' in a different, and more fundamental, sense. Classical rhetoric was primarily a theory of invention, the art of discovering contents for credible discourse about human affairs. Indeed Aristotle defined the *entire* field of rhetoric as the faculty of finding (inventing) the means of persuasion on any subject whatever.[16] Only at an advanced stage of this heuristic process does one look about for fitting language. In fact elocution is the third of five divisions of rhetorical study; *inventio* is the first. The Greco-Roman rhetors make it seem that invention was all but the queen of the rhetorical arts. The title of this paper refers not to stylistic premises but to inventional assumptions.

The pagan authorities agree on another thing: some people who have had no rhetorical schooling nonetheless have the knack for finding the means of persuasion. The textbooks were written to perfect this *ingenium* — to lift it to the level of an art, to make it transmittable, to protect it as a cultural asset. Nor did the writing of the manuals bring to an end some pristine age of *ingenium*. This natural ability, greater or less, of course, even among gifted people, remained (remains) as a fountainhead of eloquence.[17] The pre-Carolingian period of medieval history was not empty of it. Yet writers like Gregory of Tours and Bede had more than *ingenium*. Their heuristic practices were too like those of ancient rhetorical historians to have been the lucky product of hit-and-miss; from a received Latin tradition they learned, at least by fruitful observation, how to find the materials of affecting history.

In this tradition several things were assumed about historiographical *inventio*. First, that the historian marshals all his resources to win over the audience. 'The essence of the rhetorical attitude toward literature is that every form of λόγος , verse or prose, is a form of persuasion, and is to be judged by its effectiveness for this purpose', writes D.A. Russell.[18] This attitude springs from the nature of rhetorical thought: in rhetoric one *begins* with a conclusion and then proceeds by whatever means lead to it. It is otherwise in logic, where the conclusion comes last. The rhetorical attitude had immediate appeal to Christian writers, who had no want of conclusions. Indeed the Christian community existed in what might be called a continuously rhetorical situation — in perennial need of finding the means of persuading people to accept the vouchsafed truths. A cultivated persuasive purpose sets the rhetorical historian apart from the laconic annalists; or, in Cicero's terms, it separates *exornatores rerum* from *tantummodo narratores*.[19] Above all, the rhetorical historian labors to influence the thought and behavior of his reader, to teach by example. Hagiography, the most typical and beloved form of medieval literature, assured the survival of this assumption in pre-Carolingian historical writing.

Another heuristic premise of rhetorical historiography was that the historian takes a utilitarian attitude, since the valued end of his activity justifies the available means of reaching it. In all forms of historical narrative, real events were the preferred contents. But in rhetorical historiography the rule of truth is unequally yoked to a practical purpose: the historian states the facts within the limits of a persuasive program. This does not mean, of course, that the truth had no chance in rhetorical history writing; in fact it was taken for granted that *historia* was different from other forms of prose narrative precisely because it recounts *res gestae*, actual events. Yet in rhetorical historiography it is likely that one will write more, or perhaps something other, than what the gathered sources say.[20] Sources, like 'oral testimony', are not always complete and clear, let alone pre-packaged for persuasive narrative. The rhetors speak as if information about events in question will usually need some working up.

Lucian, one of the few theorists of classical historiography and a fierce advocate of the ideal of truth, makes the same assumption about the historian's materials.[21] Once he has gathered them, preferably from impartial eyewitnesses, he must go on to make them, as Lucian says, 'more credible'. This upgrading Lucian likens to sculpting: the sculptor begins with the best materials, like ivory, and then by 'fashioning', 'polishing', 'aligning', 'sawing', 'glueing', and similar techniques he brings forth a thing of moving impact. Thus the historian, on this analogy, starts with the most desirable substance, real events; but they will be of no specific use to him as an artist until he has altered them to some effect. Like the sculptor, he will define the affecting contents of an unformed mass by means of creative imagination. The schoolroom declamation cultivated this method. 'At its best', writes Kennedy, the declamation was 'an exercise of the imagination'.[22] Lucian assumes, as do the rhetors, that this imagination will normally play upon a pre-existing body of information. To hear Jerome tell it, however, declamation often taught one how to generate handy fictions. In rhetorical thought it was assumed, at any rate, that one will develop whatever contents favor the cause. This utilitarian premise was apparently well known to the early medieval forgers. The substantial narrative contained in the so-called *Donation of Constantine* is a nearly textbook-perfect example of Quintilian's *color*, the fully fictitious account composed for practical advantage. Forgery is extreme evidence of the heuristic pragmatism which generally prevailed among the more expansive and purposeful barbarian narrators.

The *Donation* won its way partly because it was internally plausible. It was not freely invented; it refers to real historical figures and states what could have happened. This reflects a third inventional premise of rhetorical historiography: that at every stage of producing the narrative the historian will apply the rule of verisimilitude. The theory of rhetorical invention is not primarily designed to discover the truth, but to find the means of persuasion. The anonymous author of the textbook *Ad Herennium* says, in fact, that there is no use telling the truth if the audience will not believe it.[23] Even the truth must meet the standard of verisimilitude, for the facts themselves may be incredible.

The great part of the inventional theory has to do with finding probable (verisimilar) contents. 'The probable', Cicero writes, 'is that which usually takes place, which is fixed in opinion, or which has some resemblance to these things, whether the resemblance is true or false'.[24] On these terms a narrative will be probable if it meets two broad tests: everyday experience and current belief.[25] It must, in the first place, recount events as ordinary people know them — with a place, a time, motives, and so on. In filling out this field of narrative circumstances, the critical concern is plausibility; whether, for example, the place was sufficient and the time opportune, is more important than what in fact these things were. Then, second, the plausible narrative must respect the popular stereotypes, mores, morals, legends, gods which people associate with life in all its dimensions. On Cicero's definition of probability, the winning narrative will be 'like the truth' as people know it, even if the likeness is an illusion. It will have, like the *narratio* in the *Donation of Constantine*, inherent probability. This is, obviously, not the probability towards which the modern historian argues. He tries to establish that an event probably took place in one way and not in any other. His narrative is written precisely to deny the empirical probability of any rivals. In rhetorical thought, as Quintilian says, the more probable does not negate the probable, any more than what is whiter contradicts what is white.[26] Indeed several alternative accounts of the same events may possess equal plausibility, but differ in details because of varying persuasive applications. This possibility Augustine saw in the four Gospels; in his view they are all credible once one views their differences as a function of four distinct instructional programs.[27] By contrast, words like 'plausibility' and 'verisimilitude' are not synonyms for the modern historian's probability. He fixes his attention on the empirical assessment of the sources; the audience is an afterthought. For the rhetorical historian, it is the other way round. He thinks first of the audience and its capacity for belief; then he chooses contents accordingly. His narrative *may* be true in his own eyes, but it *must* be credible to the audience. For all practical purposes, this plausibility is all that matters.

I might quickly mention two familiar features of early medieval historiography which show that these three inventional assumptions lived on. One is direct discourse. It continued to be a principal means by which historians instructed their readers. Yet seldom did a writer even hear the words he recorded, let alone take a transcript or make notes. Nonetheless historians often inscribed direct discourse, and the Latin rhetorical manuals help us to understand how. The rule was that one may impute speeches if they seem appropriate to the speaker and the occasion.[28] It must be credible, in other words, that such a person will have said such things in such circumstances. On these terms the historian was free to pursue his practical purpose within the limits of verisimilitude. This freedom unmistakably prevailed in another feature of pre-Carolingian historical writing, hagiographical stereotyping. Across many otherwise diverse *vitae* and *passiones*, different saints and martyrs do and say similar, even identical, things. This transferability of hagiographical phenomena was, says Père Delehaye, the idea of 'pious rhetoricians', writers who expanded their stories on terms first taught in the classical higher education.[29] The method rested in part on the apparently ageless assumption that people usually act in character. Hence Victorinus, commenting on Cicero's narrative theory, recommended that one take the common view when talking about the various recognized sorts of persons. Do not say that whores act out chastity or pimps virtue; do say that mothers love their sons, philosophers fight against the gods, old folks decline in melancholy.[30]

The cultural lore about human conduct was attractive to orators and historians partly because it had nearly automatic plausibility: here was material which people *already* believed. But stereotyping also reflects the very nature of rhetorical historiography. Unlike modern historical writing, it puts the recurrent before the unique. If one writes to teach by example, then repetitive human behaviour is the true subject matter. 'Exemplary' historiography reflects the commonplace classical belief that history tends to repeat itself. On the one hand, this cyclical view of history gave, as Quintilian observes, special power to the *exemplum*, since what happened in the past tells one what is likely to have happened in the present;[31] on the other, it all but assured that stereotyping would be widespread in Greco-Roman historical writing. Authors as different as Thucydides and Livy reduced human beings 'to types which react identically in all circumstances'.[32] In the Early Middle Ages hagiographers were only the most numerous of all the practitioners of the *exemplum* and the received rhetorical method. Perhaps biblical exegesis created an environment of thought friendly to the survival of historiographical stereotyping; the penchant for Scriptural *typus* and *figurae* encouraged people to view the present as an image of the past. Then there was *imitatio*, both the literary technique and the moral ideal, which would have had the same effect. And, of course, the notions of *typus*, *figurae*, and *imitatio* all originally sprang from the same world that produced historiographical stereotyping. In any case, to early medieval Latin narrators, no matter what the subject, the pool of precedents for human conduct of all kinds was still an irresistible source of materials for verisimilar amplification. That these Christian writers never saw that the assumption underlying rhetorical stereotyping is at odds with the linear conception of history implied in the Bible, attests to the power of the classical legacy.

I hasten to add, however, that some formative rhetorical assumptions did not get through to the first medieval historians, and partly for this reason, the question of subject matter aside, their books look greatly different from those of Greco-Roman writers. The most important of these lost premises is that the historian must fix his gaze on the horizontal plane of interacting human motives. The rhetorical textbooks help one to speak and write competently about a strictly secular world of interest. They do not rule out appeals to fate, chance, or the gods. Yet they take for granted that one will usually try to explain human events in terms of human choices. These motives are respected for their obscurity, especially by Cicero. Hence in order to be credible one must speak with some tentativeness about them. At all odds one is expected to write in a naturalistic, explanatory style — which in full flood does not appear in European historiography before John of Salisbury, and then perhaps not again until the Renaissance.[33] This *hypotaxis* was put under wraps by the Christian theology of history. Thus medieval historians like Bede found many of their answers by looking away from the horizontal line of human forces, the habitual object of the pagan historian's attention. Compared to their Greco-Roman predecessors, these writers were less in need of the hypotactical style, with its developed causal and temporal relationships. By contrast, the expository style was the necessary complement to the classical historian's field of vision. The difference lies partly in the early medieval transformation of rhetorical study. By the early seventh century the traditional schools of rhetoric were closed even in Italy.[34] Rhetorical theory survived as an aspect of grammatical education, and its public utility now lay in the various forms of Christian discourse.

Yet it is possible to overestimate this reassignment of rhetorical theory and practice. Standard authorities make it seem that by the later seventh century all of classical rhetoric but the elocutional precepts had effectively died a double death, first in the schools and then in the *scriptoria*. For Pierre Riché the writings of the Venerable Bede are the conclusive evidence for this development.[35] Even though Bede repeatedly vows to follow the footsteps of the Fathers, Riché nonetheless believes that he banished from the received patristic propaedeutics the whole of Roman rhetoric except the theory of figures. In my view Bede's writings support a very different conclusion: they tell for the theme of this essay.

Bede's attitude toward what he calls 'saecularis eloquentia' was not merely negative but deliberately ambivalent.[36] There is the well known dark side, but it never shows itself in any campaign against rhetoric itself. What bothers Bede is that bad men often use rhetoric to do mischief. Heretics are the hardies among this lot. Eloquence is to heretics, he once says, what seductive clothes are to harlots.[37] Beware of the writings of Julian of Eclanum, he warns elsewhere, for he is 'rhetor peritissimus'.[38] There is much more to this effect, but these often mentioned texts are not the whole of the evidence for Bede's attitude toward Roman rhetoric. In his view the Church cannot lay down its best verbal arms if its enemies will then have a monopoly. Once he remarkably argues, in fact, that piety and sound doctrine may not be enough when it comes to the defense of the faith. He urges that one also be prepared to fight eloquence with superior eloquence. He takes an example: at Nicaea all might have been lost if Athanasius had not known how to beat Arius at his own verbal game. In challenges of this sort one must be 'either' fortified by the truth 'or' trained to prevail in debate.[39]

Earlier in the same commentary, on I Samuel, Bede even takes Jerome to task for his famous oath recorded in Letter 22. This long and measured critique is generally a defense of reading pagan literature but specifically a call for the tactical study of rhetoric.[40] In fact Bede responds to Jerome at the very heart of Letter 22, where everything

Ciceronian or otherwise pagan is forsworn. Paraphrasing the biblical words of Jonathan, who tasted honey to good effect even though his father, King Saul, had taken an oath that no Israelite should eat till night in the land of the heathen, Bede says, 'See ... how I have become more effectual, keen, and instant to speak at length because I have tasted somewhat from the flower of a Tullian text'. In Letter 22 Jerome speaks as if the name Cicero were a synonym for killing pride. In his reply Bede endorses the reading of Cicero; actually, of all the pagan writers Jerome scores off — including Vergil, whose works Bede happily quotes more than a hundred times — he commends no author but Cicero. It is at least an extraordinary show of interest, not to say courage, especially when one comes to consider the rhetorical power of Jerome's condemnation of 'Ciceronianism'.

Bede's ambivalent attitude toward rhetoric is much like that of Augustine. In *De doctrina christiana* 4.3 Augustine observes that the art of eloquence is in itself morally neutral, useful to whatever hands take it up. It could therefore be folly if the Church forswore it, for then it might be hurt by the very weapon it had put down. Thus the Church must have eloquence in order to maintain superiority in verbal armaments.[41] Nor is there anything distinctively Christian about Augustine's view: it is an adaptation of the defense of eloquence long before mounted by the Roman rhetors.[42] Out of great respect for the imperious force of skillful language, they too were ambivalent about rhetoric, since it could be used equally well on either side of the question. Here is a basic assumption of pagan rhetoric which certainly survives in the writings of Bede.

It has recently been argued that Gildas, in the mid-sixth century, studied rhetoric in Britain with a proper rhetor.[43] Various publications make it seem that a new view of Bede's Latin culture, one which stresses his classical affinities, may be in the making.[44] I am sure that his monastic education took him into the Ciceronian inventional theory. In his first commentary on Acts, one of his earliest works, he found a factual error in Stephen's speech before the Sanhedrin: the protomartyr gave the wrong burial place for Jacob.[45] To account for it Bede first took seriously a forensic situation, since Stephen was, after all, on trial; and then he asked what courtroom orators are permitted to do. To answer this question he somehow turned to the Ciceronian rhetoric. A forensic narrative will possess verisimilitude, Cicero says in the *De inventione*, if it draws on various topics like 'the opinion of the listening audience'. Victorinus, commenting on the Ciceronian theory of probability, draws out the utilitarian attitude implicit within it; the orator, he says, will reflect the relevant audience *opinio* even when he himself does not believe it.[46] Now Bede saw Stephen's error exactly in this vein. Since Stephen was, Bede observes, speaking to the vulgar, he stated the vulgar opinion about Jacob's grave site. 'He sets his eyes less on the correct historical detail than on the case he was pleading.'[47] In other words, the truth about Jacob's grave would have been incredible to the audience; hence Stephen consciously stated an error here, to avoid damage to the plausibility of his *narratio* elsewhere. Bede wrote this exegesis of Acts 7:16 with some hesitation: 'This I have said as best I can without prejudice for a better opinion should one come along.' These reluctant words prove, I believe, that the exposition was entirely Bede's. And he had, of course, a chance to revise it, in the *retractatio* on Acts, one of his latest and most learned works. There is, however, no further thought about Stephen's apparent error, nor any hesitation about rhetorical pragmatism. Instead he praises Stephen's 'ars loquendi', as if he had now come to admire the rhetorical tactics which had earlier given him pause.[48] The entire discussion of Acts 7:16 strengthens my belief that Bede, the defender of Cicero, had actually seen something of his books, very probably the *De inventione*, or at least Victorinus' commentary on it.[49] In all the rhetorical textbook literature before Bede, the *De inventione* is the only manual which explicitly puts audience opinion among the topoi of forensic narrative. It seems very unlikely that as Bede reflected on the rhetorical foundations of Stephen's courtroom *narratio* he hit by chance on a principal of verisimilitude uniquely taught in this book.

At any rate, the exegesis of Acts 7:16 unmistakably shows that Bede's rhetorical sophistication extended to the inventional assumptions summed up earlier in this essay. Stephen's courtroom *narratio* consists of a review of Hebrew history harnessed to a practical purpose — history recounted for rhetorical impact. As Bede saw it, the narrator took a utilitarian attitude, subordinating even the truth to the end in view. And, mindful of what was fixed in the opinion of the listening audience, Stephen stated the truth insofar as it was likely to *seem* true; inherent plausibility, verisimilitude, was the final test. Nor is this the only instance in which Bede found one or more of these premises imbedded in the biblical narratives.[50] Would he have denied them to himself when he came to write the *Historia ecclesiastica*?

The practical value of history Livy described as follows: 'What chiefly makes the study of history wholesome and profitable is this, that you find the lessons of every kind of experience set forth as a conspicuous monument; and from these you may choose for yourself and your own state what to imitate, from these mark for avoidance what is shameful in the conception and shameful in the result'.[51] In the preface of the *Historia ecclesiastica* Bede took the same view: 'Should history tell of good men and their good estate, the thoughtful listener is spurred on to imitate the good; should it record the evil ends of wicked men, no less effectually the devout and earnest listener or reader is kindled to eschew what is harmful....'[52] For Bede, too, the historian writes primarily to move the audience, to teach by example. The remainder of the preface must be read in light of this rhetorical purpose.

It was written, as I have argued elsewhere, partly against Isidore's rigorous emphasis on autopsy.[53] Very little of the *Historia ecclesiastica* has to do with Bede's adult lifetime, let alone his own ocular testimony. Not much of the narrative rests on written sources; the great part of it stands on oral tradition, some of it a century old. Bede makes it known that an ecclesiastical elite helped him to gather information, written and oral. Nor does he hide the fact that these materials were collected partly, perhaps mainly, *viva voce* — by just the method Isidore writes off. It is important to remember that Bede did not impute culpable lying to Stephen when he deliberately used erroneous contents for a rhetorical purpose. In the same orbit of thought Bede asks his own readers not to blame him if in what he has written they find anything other than 'veritas', real events. 'For, in accordance with a true law of history, I have tried to set down in a simple style what I have collected from common report, for the instruction of posterity.'[54] Bede knew that Isidore's doctrine of autopsy was a fringe opinion in the tradition of Latin historiography. His 'vera lex historiae' declares a precedent in the mainstream. It affirms the premise on which Livy and others wrote the history of early Rome: that the valued ends of historical writing justify the available means of reaching them.[55] 'We are not bound to suppose that he himself believed everything he chose to record', Peter Hunter Blair says about Bede and the *Historia ecclesiastica*.[56] Indeed, his 'vera lex historiae' clearly implies that the historian is authorized to write 'ad instructionem posteritatis' even from sources which mingle truth and error. Bede took the utilitarian attitude of the rhetorical historian. As for what he himself, quite apart from the opinions of other people, thought about the factual quality of his secondhand sources, he would have judged them by the standard of inherent probability. There was no other way, and nothing more was needed. Bede says that Albinus of Canterbury, his most important source of information, sent to him materials which 'seemed' worthy of memory.[57] It was a rhetorically sophisticated choice of verbs.

After the preface comes a geographical and ethnographical excursus. This too fits the pagan rhetorical mold, even in the apparent desire to entertain with imagery to draw the eyes and the nose, oddities to test the imagination, and direct discourse to lend stylistic variety. It is a restrained replica of the rhetorical set-piece, an earnest of literary pleasure to come.[58] The overall artistic excellence of the work seems to be a growing fascination of Bedan scholars. The book is great history 'because it is great art', says Patrick Wormald.[59] Some years ago David Kirby, in a well-known essay on Bede's English sources, concluded that the *Historia ecclesiastica* has the look of an ample synthesis not because of abundant information but because of literary skill.[60] Rhetorical skill may be the better term.

At the end of a story about a certain Imma whose bonds were loosened by prayer, Bede says that he learned of this boy from people who knew him. Hence he thought it 'undoubtedly' should be put into the narrative, 'since I have so clear an account of it'. If one pauses to think how often this must not have been true of his oral sources, how often they must have been unclear and incomplete, then one can almost feel a sigh of relief wafting up from the page. It would appear that Bede's *fama* was patchy even for Northumbria and far worse for the rest of England. At the same time we know that he took a written work, the anonymous Lindisfarne *Vita Cuthberti*, and in the rewriting of it made the story twice as long. Plummer called some of this amplification 'rhetorical matter which can only be called padding'.[62] I would think that needless verbiage is the proverbial tip of the iceberg — that Bede probably wrote materially more than his supplementary oral information contained. In the added bits there is a great amount of direct discourse, the fairest of fields for imaginative reconstruction.[63] From his commentaries it is clear that he knew how to find materials for discussion of the biblical text by applying imagination to the central topoi of forensic rhetoric, the so-called 'circumstances' (who, what, when, where, and so on).[64] This method would have been no less rewarding when it came to fragmentary and confusing historical sources. He would have cast about in thought for things to add fullness and impact to the story, things which adhere credibly to the original information and help to move the reader in the desired direction. Of course he occasionally turned to written documents, above all the Bible. In rhetorical terms the Scriptures were for him a great *locus communis*, a vast and rich storehouse of contents for compelling talk about human affairs. His principal task, however, was not to ransack books but to work up oral tradition for publication in a volume of Latin historiography. It was a problem less of style than of invention. We may be sure that he augmented his oral sources for didactic effect, with materials 'like the truth'. The criteria would have been everyday life and current opinion. We readily grant this method to the early medieval hagiographers, who include, of course, Bede.[65] There is no reason to refuse it to the historians.

Let me comment on a famous part of the *Historia ecclesiastica*, the account of the Synod of Whitby.[66] It has been said that the vivid detail of the narrative, which consists almost entirely of direct discourse, attests to the graphic amplitude of oral sagas.[67] But the very short account of

Eddius Stephanus would seem to suggest something different about the scale of these unwritten stories. One might ask, too, whether doctrinal complexity, of which one finds plenty in Bede's narrative, was likely to have been a feature of sagas. I prefer to think that if Bede had had little more than Eddius' testimony, he would nonetheless have produced a vivid and detailed Whitby history. Certainly his information did not come cut already to the larger pattern of the *Historia ecclesiastica*. To find this design Bede seems to have turned to the Acts of the Apostles, a book he expounded twice, the second time while he was probably at work also on the *Historia ecclesiastica*.[68] Luke narrates the beginnings of a new church, the deeds of great evangelists, the rejection of mixed customs at a pivotal church council, the miraculous signs of God's good will toward a young Christian people, and the appearance of a missionary interest in lands across the sea. The *Historia ecclesiastica* seems to exemplify exactly these themes, even in the same order. Thus the Synod of Whitby was to Bede what the Council of Jerusalem was to Luke: the point at which a new church went on record for catholic faith. There are other points of apparent contact, including the fact that each council comes about midway in the larger narrative, as if it were a kind of fulcrum.

Hence it is all the more important to notice that when it came to the internal development of the Whitby narrative, Bede did not imitate Acts 15. The council is said to have met to consider what Bede calls 'controversia' or 'quaestio'. The pagan rhetors habitually use these words to signify a public dispute. At Whitby the speakers did not ask whether a crime had been committed but what course of action the English Church should pursue. In rhetorical language, it was an occasion for deliberative, not judicial, oratory. It is therefore striking that Bede presents the proceedings of the council in the form of matched speeches, Wilfrid advocating the Roman alternative and Colman the Irish. Paired speeches were a favourite form of Roman deliberative oratory and a preferred device of rhetorical historians. Bede presents the addresses with some rhetorical jargon; he refers, for example, to Wilfrid's 'peroratio'. But much more telling is the language he uses to speak of the assembly itself. In the early part of the narrative, before Bede has gotten to the speeches, it is called 'synodus.' But immediately after the talking is finished, he refers to it as 'contio'.[69] In classical Latin this word means 'assembly', but it was, by transference, also applied to the deliberative speeches made before assemblies. Thus these speeches were often known as 'contiones'. Bede applied the word 'contio' to an assembly in which alternating speakers discussed possible courses of public action. The word never again appears in the *Historia ecclesiastica*.[70] That Bede wrote it only here, in exactly the right context, was not the luck of high *ingenium*. It reflects a self-conscious and informed attempt to develop the Whitby narrative in the tradition of Roman eloquence. As for the learned theological and computistical contents of the paired speeches, they were not found in Eddius or the *fama vulgans*. They were, in the strict rhetorical sense, Bede's own invention. He found them by asking what arguments would have carried the day, by imagining things which could have happened on the occasion as he knew it. And all this he combined with the alluring power of cultivated Latin, to impart moral and religious truth even through literary pleasure. Bede wrote the narrative in a utilitarian attitude, with an eye on inherent probability as his audience would have recognized it.

The Whitby history is not an isolated case of rhetorical reconstruction. Wherever Bede's sources were somehow incomplete or otherwise inadequate for his instructional purpose, the same inventional method was ready to hand. From the *Historia ecclesiastica* we cannot say how ample, orderly, and didactically pointed his oral information was. But the work proves unquestionably that he was a Latin writer of great resourcefulness, one who was not likely to be defeated by *fama vulgans*. 'Bede's whole training', says Patrick Wormald, 'made him a commentator upon, rather than a recorder of, events....'[71] In Cicero's terms, Bede belongs among the *exornatores rerum*, not the mere *narratores*. What made the difference, no matter how one labels it, was rhetorical assumptions which link Cicero and Bede. They came to him through hagiographical reading and writing, biblical study, and an articulate interest in pagan eloquence as an indispensable tool of Christian education and polemics.[72] There was another medium: the Late Roman tradition of Christian historiography. It must not be forgotten that writers like Eusebius of Caesarea and Orosius, both well known to Bede, were products of the rhetorical schools; their narratives owe much to the inventional assumptions which among didactic historians of all kinds held the field from Classical Greece onwards. Bede was the best pre-Carolingian practitioner of them, but certainly not the first.

NOTES

1. *Comm. in Ep. ad Galatas*, PL 26, cols. 363–367.
2. Ep. 40, ed. A. Goldbacher, *CSEL* 34 (Vienna, 1898), pp. 71–72. On this controversy see, most recently, J.N.D. Kelly, *Jerome* (London, 1975), pp. 218–219, 263–272.
3. For the *locus classicus* see Cicero, *De or.* 2.35–63. On the relationship between rhetoric and history in classical culture, see P.G. Walsh, *Livy, His Historical Aims and*

Methods (Cambridge, 1961), pp. 20–45; T.P. Wiseman, *Clio's Cosmetics: Three Studies in Greco-Roman Literature* (Leicester, 1979), pp. 3–53, and the somewhat broader statement in his subsequent study 'Practice and Theory in Roman Historiography', *History* 218 (1981), 375–393.

4. Cicero, *De inv.* 1.9: "Inventio est excogitatio rerum verarum aut veri similium quae causam probabilem reddant...".

5. *Explanatio in rhet. Ciceronis*, ed. C. Halm, in *Rhetores Latini Minores* (Leipzig, 1863), p. 203. Cp. Quintilian, *Inst.* 2.4.2–19.

6. See D.A. Russell, 'Rhetoric and Criticism', *Greece and Rome* 14 (1967), 135–136.

7. *Inst.* 4.2.88–100.

8. *PL* 26, col. 365.

9. Esp. *Clio's Cosmetics*, pp. 3–26 (above, n. 3).

10. *Inst.* 2.4.2. Surveying the forms of narrative, he tells the rhetorician to begin with 'historica, tanto robustior quanto verior'.

11. This view he developed in *De consensu Evang.*, ed. F. Weihrich, *CSEL* 43 (Vienna, 1904); cf. R. Ray, 'Augustine's *De consensu Evang.* and the Historical Education of the Venerable Bede', forthcoming in E.A. Livingstone (ed.), *Studia Patristica*.

12. See A.J. Woodman, 'Theory and Practice in Ancient Historiography', *Bulletin of the Council of University Departments* 7 (1978), 6–8, on the interplay of fact and imagination in Thucydides.

13. On the Bible as 'privileged' history, see R.A. Markus, *Saeculum: History and Society in the Theology of St. Augustine* (Cambridge, 1970), pp. 1–21.

14. *Etym.* 1.40–44, ed. W.M. Lindsay (Oxford, 1911).

15. J. Fontaine, *Isidore de Seville et la culture classique dans l'Espagne wisigothique* 1 (Paris, 1959), pp. 180–183.

16. *Rh.* 1.2.1, trans. J.H. Freese, in *Aristotle* 22, Loeb (Cambridge, Mass., 1975).

17. See the discussion of 'traditional or natural rhetoric', a feature of all societies, in G.A. Kennedy, *Classical Rhetoric and Its Christian and Secular Tradition* (Chapel Hill, N.C., 1980), pp. 3–9; and on the persistence of rhetoric as a central force in the West, W.J. Ong, 'Foreword', in W.B. Horner (ed.), *The Present State of Scholarship in Historical and Contemporary Rhetoric* (Columbia, Mo., 1983), pp. 1–9.

18. 'Rhetoric and Criticism', p. 132 (above, n. 6).

19. *De or.* 2.54.

20. On the place of factual truth in classical historiography, see the works of Wiseman cited above (n. 3); for a very different, and less convincing, appraisal, P.A. Brunt, 'Cicero and Historiography', in *Philias charin: Miscellanea di studi classici in onore di Eugenio Manni* (Rome, 1979), pp. 311–340. Wiseman shows that rhetorical theory helps one to talk clearly about this problem in terms which Greco-Roman writers would have understood.

21. *Hist. conscr.* 47–51, trans. K. Kilburn, in *Lucian* 6, Loeb (Cambridge, Mass., 1959).

22. *The Art of Rhetoric in the Roman World* (Princeton, 1972), p. 33.

23. *Ad Her.* 1.16.

24. *De inv.* 1.46: 'Probabile autem est id quod fere solet fieri aut quod in opinione positum est aut quod habet in se ad haec quandam similitudinem, sive id falsum est sive verum'.

25. For Cicero's theory of narrative probability, see *ibid.* 1.29. Cf. S. Bonner, *Education in Ancient Rome* (London, 1977), pp. 261–263, 291–294.

26. *Inst.* 2.17.34–35: '...non autem, si quid est altero credibilius, id ei contrarium est, quod fit credibile. Nam ut candido candidius et dulci dulcius non est adversum, ita nec probabili probabilius'.

27. See Ray, 'Augustine's *De Consensu Evang.* and the Historical Education of the Venerable Bede' (above, n. 11).

28. *Ad Her.* 4.55.

29. H. Delehaye, *The Legends of the Saints*, trans. D. Attwater from the fourth revised French edition (New York, 1962), pp. 68–78.
30. *Explanatio*, pp. 206–7 (above, n. 5).
31. Inst. 3.8.66. Thus, he says, *exempla* are splendid evidence in court.
32. Walsh, *Livy*, p. 40; cf. Wiseman, *Clio's Cosmetics*, pp. 21–25 (both cited above, n. 3).
33. John of Salisbury was perhaps the only medieval historian ever to have applied the Ciceronian scepticism to the problems of historical interpretation. See R. Ray, 'Rhetorical Scepticism and Verisimilar Narrative in the *Historia Pontificalis* of John of Salisbury', in E. Breisach (ed.), *Classical Rhetoric and Medieval Historiography* (Kalamazoo, Mich., 1985), pp. 61–102. On rhetoric and history in medieval culture, see the seminal essay of J.O. Ward, 'Classical Rhetoric and the Writing of History in Medieval and Renaissance Culture', in F. McGregor and N. Wright (eds.), *European History and Its Historians* (Adelaide, 1978), pp. 1–10.
34. P. Riché, *Education and Culture in the Barbarian West, Sixth Through Eighth Centuries*, trans. J.J. Contreni (Columbia, S.C., 1976), p. 495.
35. *Ibid.*, pp. 388–393. Cf. M. Roger, *L' enseignement des lettres classiques d'Ausone à Alcuin* (Paris, 1905), pp. 394–400, for a similar opinion.
36. For a fuller account of Bede's attitude toward, and knowledge of, classical rhetoric, see R. Ray, 'Bede and Cicero', forthcoming in *ASE*.
37. *In Proverbia Salomonis libri III*, ed. D. Hurst, CCL 119B (Turnhout, 1983), p. 58.
38. *In Cantica Canticorum libri VI*, ed. D. Hurst, CCL 119B (Turnhout, 1983), p. 167.
39. *In primam partem Samuhelis libri IIII*, ed. D. Hurst, CCL 119 (Turnhout, 1962), pp. 262–263.
40. *Ibid.*, pp. 119–21. There is a detailed analysis of this remarkable passage in my 'Bede and Cicero' (above, n. 36).
41. *De doctrina Christ.*, ed. J. Martin CCL 32 (Turnhout, 1962), p. 117.
42. E.g., Cicero, *De inv.* 1.1–5.
43. M. Lapidge, 'Gildas' Education and the Latin Culture of Sub-Roman Britain', in M. Lapidge and D. Dumville (eds.), *Gildas: New Approaches* (Woodbridge, Suffolk, 1984), pp. 27–50.
44. See C. Kendall, 'Bede's *Historia Ecclesiastica*: The Rhetoric of Faith', in J.J. Murphy (ed.), *Medieval Eloquence* (Berkeley, 1978), pp. 145–72; D.K. Fry, 'The Art of Bede: Edwin's Council', in M.H. King and W.W. Stevens (eds.), *Saints, Scholars, and Heroes: Essays in Honor of Charles W. Jones* 1 (Collegeville, Minn., 1979), pp. 145–159; N. Wright, 'Bede and Vergil', *Romanobarbarica* 6 (1981), 145–162; and W. Wetherbee, 'Some Implications of Bede's Latin Style', in R.T. Farrell (ed.), *Bede and Anglo-Saxon England (British Archaeological Reports* 46, 1978), pp. 23–31.
45. *Exp. Act. Apost.*, ed. M.L.W. Laistner, in *Venerabilis Bedae Expositio Actuum Apostolorum et retractatio* (Cambridge, Mass., 1943), pp. 32–33.
46. *De inv.* 1.29; *Explanatio*, pp. 234–236 (above, n. 5).
47. *Exp. Act. Apost.*, pp.32–33: 'Verum beatus Stephanus vulgo loquens vulgi magis in dicendo sequitur opinionem; duas enim pariter narrationes coniungens, non tam ordinem circumstantis historiae quam causam de qua agebatur intendit'.
48. *Retr. in Act. Apost.*, ed. M.L.W. Laistner (above, n. 45), p. 118.
49. This I have argued in 'Bede and Cicero' (above, n. 36).
50. See Bede, *In Lucam*, ed. D. Hurst, CCL 120 (Turnhout, 1960), p. 67; and the discussion of this passage in R. Ray, 'Bede's *Vera Lex Historiae*', *Speculum* 55 (1980), 1–21. Here Bede appeals implicitly to rhetorical utility and the doctrine of verisimilitude by quoting words from Jerome's *Adversus Helvidium*. He neither names Jerome nor explains the underlying rhetorical theory — which makes it seem that he was writing for readers who knew something of rhetoric. He seems not to have seen anything of the debate between Augustine and Jerome over Galatians 2; but the

forthcoming (in *CCL*) critical edition of Bede's hitherto unpublished *Collectio* on the Pauline Epistles will decide this matter.

51. *Ab urbe condita* 1.10–11, trans. B.O. Foster, in *Livy* 1, Loeb (Cambridge, Mass., 1961).

52. *HE*, Praef., ed. and trans. B. Colgrave and R.A.B. Mynors (Oxford, 1969). This edition hereafter: *HE*.

53. Ray, 'Bede's *Vera Lex Historiae*', esp. 14–17 (above, n. 50).

54. *HE* Praef. Colgrave's translation modified.

55. See Wiseman, 'Practice and Theory in Roman Historiography' (above, n. 3).

56. 'The Historical Writings of Bede', in *La storiografia altomedievale* 1, Settimane 17 (Spoleto, 1970), p. 202.

57. *HE* Praef.: '... Albinus ... uel monimentis litterarum uel seniorum traditione cognouerat, et ea mihi de his quae memoria digna uidebantur ... transmisit.'

58. *HE* 1.1. This excursus is in fact closer to the classical tradition of the set-piece than anything in the historical works listed in M.L.W. Laistner, 'The Library of the Venerable Bede', in A.H. Thompson (ed.), *Bede: His Life, Times, and Writings* (Oxford, 1935), pp. 237–266. To write his essay Bede used, e.g., bits of a similar passage in Orosius' *Historiae*; by comparison to Bede's, Orosius' long excursus is artless and tedious.

59. 'Bede, *Beowulf*, and the Conversion of the Anglo-Saxon Aristocracy', in Farrell (ed.), *Bede and Anglo-Saxon England*, p. 69 (above, n. 44).

60. Kirby, 'Bede's Native Sources for the *Historia ecclesiastica*', *Bulletin of the John Rylands Library* 48 (1966), esp. 347, 370–371.

61. *HE* 4.22. Colgrave's translation.

62. *Bedae opera historica* 1, ed. C. Plummer (Oxford, 1896), p. xlvi.

63. Bede's *Vita Cuthberti plano sermone* is printed together with the Lindisfarne life in *Two Lives of St. Cuthbert*, ed. and trans. B. Colgrave (New York, 1939; repr. 1969).

64. See R. Ray, 'What Do We Know about Bede's Commentaries?', *RTAM* 14 (1982), esp. 16–18.

65. On rhetorical verisimilitude and hagiographical amplification, see Delehaye, *The Legends of the Saints*, pp. 68–73 (above, n. 29).

66. *HE* 3.25.

67. This is the view of N.K. Chadwick, as cited and criticized in J. Campbell, 'Bede', in T.A. Dorey (ed.), *Latin Historians* (New York, 1966), p. 164.

68. For the dates of these works see M.L.W. Laistner, *A Hand-list of Bede Manuscripts* (Cambridge, Mass. 1943), pp. 20–94. The *Retr. in Act. Apost.* and the *HE* could both have been finished in the same year. On the HE and Acts see my 'What Do We Know about Bede's Commentaries?', esp. 19–20 (above, n. 64).

69. *HE* 3.26: 'Finitoque conflictu ac soluta contione...'.

70. On *contiones* see Kennedy, *The Art of Rhetoric in the Roman World*, pp. 16–18; for *contio* in the *HE*, P.F. Jones, *A Concordance of the 'Historia ecclesiastica' of Bede* (Cambridge, Mass., 1929), p. 107.

71. 'Bede, *Beowulf*, and the Conversion of the Anglo-Saxon Aristocracy', p. 63 (above, n. 59).

72. Bede's one separate polemical work, the *Ep. ad Pleguinam* of 708, conforms well to rhetorical theory in Cicero's *De inv.*; see my 'Bede and Cicero' (above, n. 36).

ETHNIC HISTORY AND THE CAROLINGIANS: AN ALTERNATIVE READING OF PAUL THE DEACON'S *HISTORIA LANGOBARDORUM*

Donald Bullough

Theodor Mommsen was not, in my experience, a man much given to lyrical writing. But in his study of the sources of Paul the Deacon's *Historia Langobardorum*, which still retains much of its value 105 years later, he comes as near to lyricism — and occasionally absurdity — as perhaps he ever did:

It is difficult to judge of the spiritual gifts of those men who have worked on the incunabula of historiography, as difficult as it is to form a correct judgement from the works of primitive sculptors and painters with regard to the artistic capabilities of the master. But without doubt Paul has a very special place in literary history, in that Roman culture is embodied in him to an extent that no-one else attained in this period. Admittedly he wrote the Latin of his own time ... [including] the accusative absolute and the participle as substantive out of context. But anyone who has even a nodding acquaintance with the halting and bungling writings (*stammelnden und stumperhaften Schriftstücke*) composed at that time must look with amazement and at times with admiration at his always clear and generally correct Latin, his judicious sentence structure, free from all affectation, and his talent for form and style. Quite apart from the content of his narrative, it is well worth our giving thought to the way in which, putting together his History from the most disparate elements, he has given it a unity both of form and of style.... It is remarkable how he has managed to mould together the pulpit-style of Orosius, the anecdotal forms of *exempla*, the information in Roman, Frankish and Lombard annals and histories and the crude legends of the Lombard *Origo* and has in some degree tuned them up and tuned them down into a Eutropian melody.... This involves a knowledge of and interest in classical literature such as does not occur again in the same breadth and fulness before the time of the Humanists.... This vigour of a classical-Roman culture was combined in Paul with an earnest national feeling which was increased rather than diminished by the collapse of the Lombard kingdom. He has written under these influences and even to-day his pages show the double imprint of a classical formation and national feeling.[1]

Paul's Latinity, to which Mommsen gives an uncertain good mark, is not our real concern here. I note merely that more cautious and, in this matter, more analytic but non-structuralist commentators in recent decades have characterised it roughly as 'reflecting the language and patterns of Silver-Latin prose with patristic and post-patristic lexical and syntactical features' but none the less (in Professor Norberg's words) 'welding together the disparate elements to create a style that is new, personal and cultivated'.[2] Mommsen's comparison of a passage in Gregory of Tours' *Historia Francorum* with its re-handling by Paul does indeed show up the 'vulgarity' of the former — writing, however, two centuries previously; and Paul's 'improvements' significantly change the sense of the passage.[3] If he had come nearer to Paul's own time and compared him with Bede — the Bede of the *Historia Ecclesiastica*, whose narrative prose, resonant with the language of the Vulgate and of the earliest Latin 'ecclesiastical histories', most of us will continue to prefer — he could not properly have spoken of 'halting and bungling writings'. But it is time to return to Paul the historian and, in so far as it is relevant to his historical writing, to Paul the man.

Few letters of Paul have been preserved — five at the most and two of those dedication-prefaces of books. The incidental references to himself in his prose writings and 'autobiographical' passages in his poems of the 760s, 770s and 780s mean, however, that we are rather better informed about his life and career than for almost any other non-royal figure in that century, although 'absolute' dates are hard to come by.[4] He was born in the 720s or a little later into a Lombard landowning family in north-east Italy (Friuli) whose *genealogia* he believed he could trace back to the ancestor who actually arrived there from Pannonia in 568/9: although as he only allows for four generations this is not easy to credit. As an adolescent he was at the Lombard royal court, then normally resident in the palace at Pavia, during the reign of King Ratchis (744–9). There he had as his *preceptor* a certain Flavianus of whom nothing is known except for the name of his uncle: it is generally assumed that he was a grammarian and a layman; but neither proposition, however reasonable, is established by the passage in question. Where he was in the 750s, the decade of the first Carolingian invasions of the Lombard kingdom, he nowhere indicates. But he clearly managed to extend his book-learning, write his first surviving poem — the highly accomplished *Ordiar unde tuas laudes, o maxime Lari?* in praise of Lake Como and apparently composed 'sur le motif'[5] — and (most importantly) successfully negotiate a change of ruling dynasty. For before 763 he had accompanied king Desiderius' daughter to Benevento as bride of its cultivated duke Arichis; and in a letter-preface of that year he implies that he had for some time been instructing her to a surprisingly high level of education. The circumstances in which he left the ducal court are nowhere alluded to. But three of his poems read together are good evidence that some time in the 770s he left the secular world for a monastery, originally reluctantly and regretfully, and that that monastery was Monte Cassino (on the northern edge of duchy), not — as Traube thought — northern Italian Civate. It was certainly from Monte Cassino that he set out for the Carolingian Court in 782 to seek the release from captivity of his brother whose involvement in a rebellion against the Frankish conquerors in 776 had brought destitution to his wife and children. He was to stay there for only four years, although he remained in contact with it after his return to his now beloved South Italian community.[6]

Two of his asides in the *Historia Langobardorum*, both of them (I shall suggest) as revealing in what they leave unsaid as in what they say, establish that it was written after his time in Francia. The first of these is when he is contrasting the lengths of shadows at mid-day in the mid-winter in Italy and the north and records that: 'when I was staying (*al.* stationed, *constitutus*) in Belgic Gaul in a place which is called *Villa Totonis* (Thionville) and measured the shadow of my stature, I found it to be nineteen and a half feet'. By a fortunate chance a letter written to the abbot at Monte Cassino and the Frankish Royal Annals in conjunction enable us to date this stay to Christmas/New Year 782–3. In the last book of the *Historia Langobardorum*, he refers to another of his historical writings, his *Gesta* of the (arch) bishops of Metz, written at the request of the then incumbent Angilramn. Internal evidence in that work shows it to have been in progress not earlier than the late summer of 783, while leaving it open whether it was completed before Angilramn's death in 784.[7]

Anno domini datings for such episodes are, of course, hardly to be expected even if Paul had been as interested in chronology as Bede — which, demonstrably, he was not. But if *we* can calculate a fairly precise *terminus post quem* for the composition of the Lombard History from these passages, and make the further inference that it belongs to the final phase of Paul's life when he was back at Monte Cassino (*post* 786/7) and in the seventh decade of his life, we should not forget that almost no early reader could have done any such thing. In the ninth century as in the twentieth it would have been possible to read the *Historia Langobardorum* almost without realising that when Paul wrote it the Lombard Kingdom had been subjected to the Carolingian Franks for more than a decade. Almost, however, but not quite. There is a single passage – commonly overlooked by scholars since Mommsen who have proposed alternative interpretations of Paul's attitudes and purpose — which makes it clear that the Lombards are no longer an independent *gens*. In Bk.V *c.* 6 Paul adds to the brief account of the Emperor Constans II's invasion of Italy in 663, which he has taken over from the *Liber Pontificalis*, a story of Constans' visit to a certain hermit who was said to have the spirit of prophecy. 'Could he overcome the *gens Langobardorum*?' 'No', was the answer after a night's prayer, 'because a certain queen coming from another region has built the church of St John the Baptist in their territory, so that St John continually intercedes for them'. 'But' (he added cheerfully) ' a time will come when this place of prayer (*oraculum*) will be held in contempt and then that people shall perish'. The reference is, of course, as Paul himself makes clear in the next sentence, to queen Theudelinda's foundation at Monza (where, amidst furniture factories and motor-racing track, her treasures but not her building are still to be found). 'We have proved that that happened, having seen how – before the ruination of the Lombards – this same church of St John was managed by vile persons who bestowed it on the unworthy and adulterous, as if they were disposing of spoils'.[8]

The word I have translated as 'ruination', *perditio*, is one of those classified by the Utrecht School as a 'semi-Christianism', that is to say, not recorded before the Fathers although having no specifically Christian connotation: in the earliest examples it almost always refers to the fate of an individual, with an implication of self-destruction, usually through sin. Signorina Rossetti, in her excellent study of the Monza area in the Lombard and Carolingian periods, has shown how the evidence of documents from the last six years of the independent kingdom is wholly compatible with the picture given by Paul.[9] But in the present context it is the allusion to the downfall of the *gens* that is crucial.

A more oblique, one might even say 'coded', reference to the independence of the Lombards in Italy as past and gone is to be found in the very first chapter, which in the prefatory *capitula* is entitled: 'On Germany, which nourishes very many human beings, so that many peoples have migrated from it'. Paul remarks on the material destruction which migrating Germanic tribes, named and un-named, have brought to 'unhappy Italy'. But there is one more tribe from the region 'which afterwards ruled happily in Italy' (*in Italia feliciter regnavit*) — namely, of course, that of the Lombards.[10] I shall return to this passage.

Clearly apparent, surely, to a reader who comes to the *Historia Langobardorum* from almost any other Late-Antique or Early-Medieval narrative history is its oddness of structure, or (as some may prefer) its odd proportions. It is divided into six Books, with very uneven numbers of chapters, the *argumenta* of which, at the beginning of each book, are unquestionably the work of Paul himself.[11] (Does this practice go back any further in historiography than Gregory of Tours's *Historia Francorum*, where they are much more succinct?) The first book, almost exactly a sixth of the whole, begins with the already-quoted chapter *De Germania* where the Lombards are introduced in the final sentence. This leads naturally into the first of 26 further chapters which take the history of the *gens*, with digressions into other Germanic and Imperial history (plus Benedict and his monastic foundation at Monte Cassino), to the Lombard defeat of the Gepids — dated by modern scholarship to 567. Book II moves back in time a few years to provide a fairly comprehensive account of the career of the representative of Imperial authority in Italy at the time of the Lombard invasion, which Paul exceptionally dates precisely to April 568; and then reports the history of the Lombards in the peninsula over a period of six years only with a brief glance at the next decade (574–584). The third Book merely advances the story to 590–591 (the dates are modern historians', not Paul's). Book IV covers the next seventy years, Book V the period 661–680. The final Book VI regresses briefly into the 670s and then continues to the last years (but not death) of king Liutprand, sc. 742–44.

The oddities and anomalies extend to the contents of the several Books. In Book I Paul has just begun his account of the wanderings of the Lombards southwards from the Baltic or North Sea when he introduces into his German setting a version of 'the Seven Sleepers of Ephesus' — seven men in a long sleep, perfectly preserved, Roman in dress, who perhaps one day will convert the pagan peoples (*gentes*) by their preaching. The tribe in that area is named as the *Scritobini*, for which Paul provides quite a respectable Germanic etymology: but what follows is obviously intended as an account of the Finns or Lapps hunting reindeer, which Paul has taken from an unknown source.[12] Book II chs. 2–5 trace the career of Narses in the context of sixth-century Imperial history, almost without reference to the Lombards whether as allies or enemies; while chs. 14–24 (except the opening words of 14) are a catalogue or description of the provinces of Italy. The opening chapters of Book III link military campaigns by Franks, Lombards and others in a broad narrative without dates. The later chapters are equally indifferent to years but include a number of month/day dates and among them the only exact day of death of a Lombard King — Authari on 5 September (590). Many chapters are short and terse, 'looking in fact' (it has been said recently) 'very much as if they had been excerpted from a chronicle similar to that written by Marius of Aventicum (Avenches) in the late sixth century'; while two consist in their entirety of letters written by

Pope Gregory I respectively to queen Theudelinda, king Agilulf and duke Arichis of Benevento.[13]

For much of the *History* whole areas of the *regnum Langobardorum* are totally or substantially ignored: notably Tuscany (the land south and west of the Appennines to the frontier with the *Romani* north of Rome), which makes a fleeting appearance in one of the annalistic entries in Book IV, gets an incidental mention in connection with the conquest of Liguria in ?643 and then disappears completely except for an even more incidental reference to the participation of *Tusci Langobardi* in a defensive campaign in the 720s.[14] Without the remarkable series of documents from the eighth-century onwards which chance has preserved at Lucca we would know as little about this area as we do, say, of Reggio or Parma or Genoa in the Lombard period.[15] By contrast, events and leaders in the north-east of the peninsula are recorded in fair detail, although very unevenly — the succession of the dukes of Friuli, for example, and some of their heroic and not-so-heroic achievements in campaigns against both internal and external enemies. Successive bishops of Aquileia (to whom Paul anachronistically gives the title *patriarcha*) are meticulously recorded, with their years of office, until the early seventh century but not thereafter until the early eighth. Eight patriarchs of Constantinople are named but only three bishops of Pavia. The 'Christianity' of the Lombards is treated in a very peculiar way. Its beginnings are simply ignored; the first conversion of a Visigothic prince from Arianism is noted, although Paul — usually so interested in Germanic tribal names — speaks only of *Hispani* or (eventually) *Hispani Gothi*; King Rothari's Arianism is commented on; but the conversion of the Lombards to orthodoxy is never mentioned. If it had figured in Paul's narrative, we might well have been deprived of the late G.P. Bognetti's 500 pages on 'Sta Maria di Castelseprio e la storia religiosi dei Longobardi'; and the post-Second World War historiography of the Lombards would have been simpler, shorter but certainly duller.[16] What does interest Paul, to an extent which is without parallel in any other historian, is the founding or building of churches at Pavia and in one or two places elsewhere (notably Monza) — for which indeed he is a major source.[17]

Do such unbalances, omissions and apparent anomalies merely reflect the sources available to Paul when he came to write? or do they provide pointers to the overall purpose, the *Tendenz*, of the History? There has been a tendency (in another sense) in recent decades for historians of the Early and High Middle Ages to take up the most unpromising contemporary writings, repudiate the dismissive views of their predecessors on the grounds that they have asked the wrong questions, and extract from them a more or less coherent vision of the events, men and the material world of their own day, not to speak of Eternity. Much of this seems to me to do more credit to scholars' sentiment than to their intellect: they would be far less generous to an undergraduate essay handled in a similar way; and they presuppose a consistency and coherence of thought in those writers (although Michael Wallace-Hadrill deems them to be 'a rum lot') which I fail to find in most of my colleagues and would hesitate to claim for myself. I am reluctant, therefore, to play a similar game with Paul's text. But this is, after all, the primary and often the only written source for the history of the Lombards or of the Italian peninsula over two centuries, and we cannot ignore Paul's statements even when we most distrust them.

The greatest single problem of evaluation, it seems to me, is the character and significance of the material taken from non-written sources. It has long been accepted, it is hardly possible to deny, that much of what Paul reports of events before (as well as in) his own lifetime had never previously been recorded in writing, although specific references to traditional-oral material are few and generally not introduced to justify or authenticate statements in the main historical narrative.[18] There is also no dispute that at least one of Paul's written sources, which he refers to as the 'prologue of the Edict which king Rothari composed of the laws of the Lombards' and which we know as the *Origo gentis Langobardorum* — whether or not the extant manuscripts preserve it in the precise form known to Paul — is the work of an anonymous precursor who in the middle years of the seventh century wrote down a briefer account of his people's early wanderings, leaders, kings and their battles which had previously been transmitted only orally.[19] The concept of 'oral tradition' is unfortunately a loosely, even recklessly, used one, especially by historians forced (or eager) to suspend their normal critical judgement. Yet unless we can identify more precisely the 'oral' elements in the *Historia Langobardorum* and define the probable channels of their transmission to Paul, we cannot convincingly draw on his work for our kind of history.[20] The possibility of a more discriminating approach is offered by the now-considerable body of ethnographic and anthropological literature which analyses the different forms and purposes of 'oral tradition' in pre-literature societies and their implications for diachronic studies. Inevitably no one classification or typology commands universal assent, but several suggested subdivisions have proved acceptable as working tools;[21] and although our categories and distinctions will not have been Paul's, he can hardly have been unaware of differences between the informants who provided him with his 'oral' material.

Applied, then, to the *Historia Langobardorum*: there are, on the one hand, the simple factual statements — names of men and women, the events with which they are associated and so on — without literary embellishment, which will have reached a recorder from a number of different informants and transmitters but are accepted as 'literally true': the names of Paul's ancestors, for example,[22] or the names of dukes of Friuli and (less consistently) of other city-territories, and some at least of the battles or campaigns in which they participated. On the other hand, there are the truncated accounts or elaborated stories of the distant and not-so-distant Lombard past where Paul and an anonymous seventh-century writer before him have indeed recorded, through the medium of translation, 'oral literature': the wanderings and wars of the *gens* in the East European plain; Alboin's quarrel with the Gepids, his marriage to the defeated king's daughter Rosamund, her cruel revenge and equally cruel death; or the complicated and sometimes confused story of Grimoald which first surfaces in the latter part of BkIV and weaves its way through much of BkV, taking its hero from boyhood in Friuli to the dukedom of Benevento and thence to the throne of the kingdom. An earlier generation of historians and text-critics labelled the whole corpus undiscriminatingly as 'saga-material', in which the notion of a free form of text through the medium of prose is presumably implicit.[23] Ethnographers have now invited us to distinguish between (for example) 'historical' tales, didactic tales or 'testimonies designed to instruct' — often embodying aetiological myths — and tales whose primary or overriding purpose is to please the audience, whether they are (in our terms) epic or fable. Regardless of the ultimate validity of such categorisations, the student of early medieval texts must take account of one ethnologist's belief that '*because* of their intentionally historical nature, tales are generally *less* trustworthy than other types of [oral] source' (my italics);[24] but he is also bound to pose the question, even where positive evidence is lacking, whether historical and other tales were the responsibility of specialist transmitters within a specific social context.

Paradoxically, it is often the simple factual statements which are most easily tested and at times rejected by our own critical methods, even where there is no evidence to be found in an independent source. I have already suggested that Paul's account of his ancestors does not seem to have enough generations to reach back to the time of the invasion of Italy: although whether a name has dropped out, two generations have been telescoped or the first named ancestor is spuriously associated with the events of 568 — like those inhabitants of Tayside who regularly claim that a grandparent or great-uncle saw or fortuitously escaped the Tay Bridge disaster — we shall never know. Occasionally, however, other evidence does exist which points to a more elaborate example of 'false memory'. A particularly striking example is the tale, which may or may not have reached Paul as part of the 'Grimoald story', of the killing of Taso son of duke Gisulf by 'Gregory the patrician of the Romans' (by which Paul seems to mean *exarch*). The seventh-century Burgundian writer known as Fredegarius has a related story, in a context which dates it to 630/631, of the Lombard king Arioald's successful conspiracy with the patrician Isaac to kill duke Taso of Tuscany at Ravenna. Thomas Hodgkin, following contemporary German scholarship, concluded that either Fredegarius had got hold of an inaccurate version of events or the coincidence of the name Taso is accidental and there were two separate incidents some years apart. But there is no room in the succession of exarchs in early seventh-century Italy for an otherwise unknown Gregory: while Isaac was in that office and Arioald was king in 630–1. Only an excessive respect for 'tradition' or for Paul as a recorder of his people's past can explain the discounting of Fredegarius' strictly contemporary account.[25]

To what extent, then, are Paul's fuller versions of episodes and events previously recorded in more summary or divergent form in the *Origo* (at least in the only text-version that has survived) dependent on traditions or literature that were circulating orally in Paul's lifetime? and how far had any current oral material itself been influenced by earlier written versions? There can be no entirely persuasive answer to either question: the only independent evidence of early date for a Lombardic oral and literary tradition is the Old High German *Hildebrandslied* ('the only surviving heroic lay recorded in German'), or more precisely the belief of many scholars that the 'first version of the poem was ... composed in [the Lombard kingdom] in the seventh or eighth century and grafted on to the Dietrich legend'.[26] Mommsen's solution was to suppose that the primitive text of the *Origo* was much fuller than the surviving versions and that its original form can be largely reconstructed from the *Historia Langobardorum*. He has not found many supporters, although some of his most vigorous opponents have not helped their case by postulating a second written account of the early history of the Lombards of which there is no trace elsewhere![27] In one passage Paul does seem to be hinting at an awareness of alternative traditions: but if that is the correct understanding of his words, his reaction is an interesting one. The passage already quoted where Paul names the Rothari-Edict prologue as a source is introduced by the words 'if anyone thinks [that my account of the defeat and exile of Tato's son Hildechis as the cause of later emnity between Gepids and Lombards] is a fiction and not the truth of the matter (*si quis mendacium et non rei existimat veritatem*) let him read that prologue': adding somewhat unexpectedly — if I am translating correctly — 'and he will find it in almost all manuscripts (*codicibus*)' of the Laws.[28]

Where appropriate written sources were available and accessible (in Latin, that is; for Procopius, who would have been invaluable, was literally a closed book to him), he was only too happy to use them, even if they conflicted with what he had learned from 'oral tradition' or even with one another: reconciling chronological data was not a problem that ever engaged him. The detailed narrative (with dates) in the later chapters of Book III and in Book IV from ch.9 onwards is substantially from abbot Secundus of Trento's otherwise-lost *succincta de Langobardorum gestis historiola*, which included the record of a personal visit to Monza in 603. This has long been recognised as the only plausible source for the detailed account of events in the valleys of the river Adige and its tributaries in 590, and more recently claimed as Paul's source for the controversial statement earlier in Book III (ch.16) that 'the oppressed people *per Langobardos hospites partiuntur*'.[29] The possibility of a different north-Italian annalistic text in which Paul found the statements incorporated in his equally-controversial Book II ch.32, and in which the compiler of the *Origo* before him found his precise date — *mense Aprilis a pascha indictione prima* — for the beginning of the invasion, has several times been raised but never resolved. (There are noteworthy links between the *Origo* and Marius of Avenches's contemporary account of the murder of Alboin in 572 but not between their respective accounts of the invasion.) Paul apparently did not know, he certainly did not use, any version of the extant annals kept probably at Milan or Pavia which date the succession and death of early-seventh-century Lombard kings.[30] It is possible, but not absolutely demanded by his text, that he had an episcopal list for the see of Aquileia, independent of any information in Secundus: if, however, the sequence of bishops of Pavia was recorded in the diptychs or a manuscript in that city, it is apparent that Paul made no use of it.[31] He must have read at least one Lombard king-list, namely the seventeen names included at Rothari's command — *in quantum per antiquos homines didicimus* — in the Prologue proper of his Edict; but he did not include its genealogical statements in his own work and he similarly ignored Rothari's own twelve-generation patriline genealogy.[32]

What strikes me forcibly in this broad conspectus of Paul's sources — and of those he might have used but didn't — is that there is nothing in the putatively oral element that does not obviously belong to the earliest phases of his life, i.e. his childhood with his family in Friuli and his adolescent years at the Pavian Court. Lombard relations with their aggressive Slav neighbours are updated to duke Ratchis's time (*a.*744/5, therefore); the only detailed account of a battle not in Italy north of the Po is one fought on or near the most northerly section of the Via Flaminia in which Ratchis was the hero, four or five years before he became king; the passage where Paul confirms tradition from first-hand knowledge shows him acquiring it at Ratchis's Court.[33] When Desiderius returned to Pavia as king after an admittedly-brief stay in Tuscany, he apparently brought no additional traditions, local or 'national', with him. Paul's transfer to south-Italian Benevento may have provided him with the names of local dukes previously unknown to him, as well as a knowledge of Theuderata's foundation of the conventual church of S. Pietro fuori le mura in the late-seventh century (his only reference to a church in that city, although in the late 760s Paul was helping, through his verse-tituli, to make both Benevento and Salerno as much like Pavia as possible): but as Theuderata was the daughter of a Friulian duke and her husband was king Grimoald's son even that is not inevitable.[34]

The one substantial overlap between Paul's *Historia Romana* and his *Historia Langobardorum* seems strikingly to confirm the unique importance of his pre-Beneventan years for the content of the later work. In both Histories Paul connects the beginning of the destructive conflict between Lombards and Gepids with the time of Kings Audoin and Thurisind and a fatal encounter between their sons Alboin and Turismod. Crivellucci, the last and best editor of the *Historia Romana*, associates the relevant passage there with *Origo c. 5*, but that text knows nothing of the episode. Paul would have found a brief account of a bloody encounter between Gepids and Lombards (without their respective leaders' names) at the end of Jordanes's *Romana*, and reference to earlier kings, but not to Audoin's contemporary, in his *Getica*: and that is all. The only detailed contemporary account of relations between the two barbarian peoples and the only independent evidence for the Gepid king Thurisind is in Procopius' History of the Gothic Wars, where nothing is said — or even hinted at — about the part played by sons of the rival leaders.[35] Either Paul had found the names and at least the outline of the story in one of his 'lost' written sources, the *historiola* of Secundus of Trent or the putative longer version of the *Origo*, or he had acquired them from the mouth of a 'teller of tales' in the Lombard royal city. Both because of my belief that such narrative passages are unlikely to have figured in Secundus' work and my doubts whether the extended *Origo* ever existed, strengthened by the anachronistic 'social-anthropological' features in the story (to which I shall return), obviously I favour the second view.

But why was Paul the recipient of so much 'oral tradition' that would have been lost for ever if he had not subsequently written it down? My answer is a simple but speculative one — speculative but entirely compatible with the evidence that he himself provides: namely, that the young Warnefrid, of impeccably Lombard ancestry and apparently with an interest already in family genealogy and possibly in the heroic doings of the contemporary duke of Friuli and some of his predecessors, was acknowledged at Court (perhaps even brought there) as the next link in a chain of oral transmission: that is to say, he was an exact counterpart among the Lombards of the young Icelandic story-teller who, as he told King Harald Hardrada (c. 1050), had learnt the *Útferfa saga* over several summers at the Althing from the mouth of the King's own follower Halldór Snorrason.[36]

Paul's vernacular culture was soon overlaid by a Latin one: and, as we know, to excellent effect. But comparison of the writings certainly used by Paul to create an expanded and partially-Christianised *Historia Romana* from Eutropius' text with the identifiable written sources of the *Historia Langobardorum* makes a similar point to that suggested by the oral elements: most of those he used in the later work were ones he certainly knew or would most easily have found before he left the Lombard Court — not only Secundus' *succincta historiola*, the botched *Catalogus provinciarum Italiae*,[37] the *Origo* and manuscripts of Rothari's Edict, but also the *Liber Pontificalis* and Pope Gregory's Dialogues. Indeed, his letter dedicating the Roman History to Adelperga concludes with a promise that, having brought it down to the time of Justinian, he will continue it 'to our own time' if that is what she wants and if *maiorum dicta* (sayings? or written texts?) offer the necessary support.[38]

In the event, Paul only composed the second part of his historical diptych 25 or 30 years later, in very different circumstances and stopping a full half-century before 'our own time'. He had sought the Court of an alien monarch, the conqueror of his people, the captor of his brother, from family duty. Initially it was an uncongenial atmosphere, in spite of the presence there of Italians and others who shared some of his cultural interests. His one surviving letter from this phase of his life, written to the abbot of Monte Cassino in the opening weeks of 783, declares that 'he had been well-received and was being well treated: but in comparison with that community the court was a prison'; and he longed for the *otium* of the monastic life. A new and fine study of Carolingian Court poetry detects a growing warmth towards the Frankish king.[39] This is certainly in line with the evidence of intimacy with Charles, comparable to that with Ratchis 40 years earlier, in Paul's *Gesta* of the Bishops of Metz;[40] and it accords with the view, which has been widely accepted since Mommsen, that he deliberately ended his History of the Lombards with the reign of the last king who was not in conflict with the Pope and with the Franks — thus avoiding having to commemorate an admired Frankish king as the instrument of the destruction of his people. The fact remains, however, that Paul left the Frankish Court after only four years, just as the circle of scholars and literary men there was beginning to widen and as books were being acquired. Back in Italy, it is true, Paul supplied king and Court with both liturgical and grammatical texts, partly on request and partly (it seems) on his own initiative: and poems continued to be addressed to him in the king's name, the latest almost certainly composed by Alcuin.[41] But could it be that it was the king who was displaying the greater regard and affection?

For if Paul combined regret at his people's loss of independence with admiration for its Frankish conqueror and his establishment of a new Christian *pax*, as many in the Court circle would certainly have claimed, he could easily have demonstrated this at several points in his Lombard History without stylistic infelicities. He did no such thing. The Franks figure in his narrative almost entirely as enemies.[42] A digression on Arnulf of Metz, chronologically out of place and concentrating on his spiritual qualities — for which there was probably no evidence worth the name — is admittedly introduced by the statement that it was to the *maiores domui* that royal power among the Franks was eventually transferred; but the opportunity of telling readers who is now the distinguished representative of that line is not taken. When Paul records the length of his shadow at Thionville, he does not tell us that he was there with the king and his Court.[43] And in the very first chapter of the *Historia Langobardorum*, as we have seen, he contrasts the succession of barbarian peoples from Germany, including some unnamed, who have brought misery and destruction to Italy with his own Lombards who alone ruled it happily.

This is not to say that Paul's years at the Frankish Court had a purely negative effect on the achievement of his old age. We have good reasons for believing that it was only there that Paul read an earlier History, and possibly other works too, which helped to determine the form and structure of his account of the Lombard past. Gregory of Tours' *History of the Franks* is used already in Book II of the *Historia Langobardorum* in ways that suggest that it would have provided material for the end of Book 15 and the beginning of Book 16 of the *Historia Romana* if Paul had known it at the time; it is the textual source of the greater part of the early chapters of Book III which are not dependent on Secundus and is used alternately with the latter for many subsequent chapters. These are part of the process of putting the history of the *gens* in a wider context, of which the 'Imperial' chapters are another aspect: but they also provide details of the *gens* in action under the leadership of both dukes and kings which Paul had clearly not found elsewhere.[44] It would be too much to hope that the manuscript of Gregory which Paul read at this time had survived, and it hasn't: but almost certainly we have, in Monte Cassino cod. 275, a direct if defective copy of the mid-eleventh century. For this is one of the books which abbot Desiderius 'ordered to be made' from older

examplars in the library of the community; and its closest relatives
textually are eighth- and ninth-century manuscripts from northern and
eastern France.[45]

A second major work that may have come to Paul's notice for the first
time when he was at the Court in Francia is Bede's *Historia Ecclesiastica*.
It is true that Crivellucci supposed that it had already been used by him
for his *Historia Romana*: but only one of the passages he cites cannot be
adequately or better explained as depending on Bede's Chronicle with
Paul's characteristic verbal modifications; the likelihood that he would
have drawn on the Ecclesiastical History for events on the Continent in
the fifth century rather than on contemporary annalistic works which he
was demonstrably using for preceding and succeeding passages does not
seem very great; and it may indeed be doubted whether Bede's History
was already available in Benevento in the 760s.[46] One late chapter of the
Historia Langobardorum, namely VI 17, is taken almost in its entirety
from Bede's account of the abdication and burial in Rome of king
Caedwalla of Wessex. Paul postulates a link with the Lombard king
Cunincpert, which provides him with an excuse for introducing that
episode into his narrative; but I suspect that what had attracted him to
the passage in the Ecclesiastical History was the recording of Caedwalla's
poetic epitaph. Professor Bischoff has shown that the distinctive hand of
an early addition to the Northumbrian 'Moore' manuscript of the
Historia Ecclesiastica is evidence of its presence at the Frankish Court in
the last years of the eighth century, whether or not Alcuin and his
northern-English circle were responsible for bringing it there. The
tempting and natural inference that this was the book actually read by
Paul is, however, made unlikely by a distinctive reading in the epitaph
where Paul and the Bede-manuscript diverge.[47]

Whenever and wherever Paul first became acquainted with Bede's
great book, it surely also provided the 'model' or stimulus for what is
otherwise an unexpected and anomalous feature of the *Historia
Langobardorum*: namely, the insertion of three letters of Pope Gregory I
in (typically) erroneous chronological contexts. Since, in the course of his
return journey to Monte Cassino through north Italy (786–7?), Paul had
a copy made of a small and distinctive collection of the Pope's letters for
abbot Adalhard of Corbie, it might be expected that this provided him
with the texts. In fact it didn't: all three letters occur only in a quite
different collection, preserved in three ninth-century copies whose origin
and provenance make it almost certain that Paul took his texts from their
archetype or a lost earlier copy while he was at Charles's court.[48]

One work of Classical Antiquity germane to Paul's purpose *may*
likewise have become available to him for the first time during his stay in
Francia: namely, the early books of Pliny's Natural History which he

knew under the title of *De Natura rerum*. But it would be rash to insist that he could not have read it before or after this time in his native Italy because there is no identifiable branch of the tradition there between the palimpsests of Late Antique manuscripts and the High Middle Ages.[49]

What, then, when Paul finally sat down at the age of sixty-plus to write a history of the Lombards, did he do with this disparate body of material, garnered at different stages of an unsettled life? He wrote what he said he was writing: the history of a *gens* from its remote origins to the point at which it was beginning to lose its separate identity, and he tackled his subject in a way that neither Gregory nor Bede had or could have done. Indeed, if Paul had a recognisable progenitor it would surely be Jordanes 'on the origin and deeds of the Getae from olden time to the present day, descending through the generations of the kings';[50] but if Mommsen were right in claiming that Paul knew the *Getica* (which was available on both sides of the Alps at the turn of the century), he made surprisingly little use of it.

Like Jordanes and Bede, but unlike Gregory, Paul begins with a geographical and ethnological introduction. Bede, however, treats here of Britain before the coming of the English, not the homeland or pre-history of these Germanic migrants: all he can offer on *origines* is the brief and notorious Book I ch.15, which reports the situation (as Bede understood it) in the early/mid-fifth century. Gregory, not having previously covered earlier ages in 'universal chronicle', properly begins his narrative with the history of salvation in 23 chapters. The Franks make their first appearance well on into Book II, as third-century enemies of the Romans: before that they have no history. When, later, the Franks had to be provided with a more ancient past this was done by linking their beginnings with the Troy legend: modern scholarship has rejected this comforting fiction without finding anything to put in its place.[51] Paul, from his distinctive geographical starting-point — *De Germania* — proceeds in his first Book as it were in parallel with his expanded 'Roman History'. When the latter comes to an end in the mid-sixth century, the parallelism between Lombard and Imperial history is maintained *within* the structure of the *Historia Langobardorum*. But the comparisons with the entire work which I suggest Paul was inviting his future readers, the élite *litterati* of Italy and Francia, to make for themselves were the existing Histories of the Franks and of the English, and especially the first of these.

In this design, the anecdotal ethnological passages have a distinctive but perfectly proper and distinctive place. Almost without exception and sometimes quite explicitly, they serve to illustrate some feature of the *gens* — its social structure, its laws, its *rites de passage*: during the Migrations slaves are freed (so that they can bear arms) *more solito per sagittam, inmurmurantes ob rei firmitatem quaedam patria verba*; the young Alboin, even after his success in combat, cannot be immediately allowed to join his father at the top table *ne ritum gentis infringeret*; and so on. It does not matter whether the recorded episodes are historically authentic or not: we shall never know, and I would guess that the *ritus gentis* in relation to royal sons belongs rather to the period of an established royal line in Italy.[52] But Paul, like many ethnological recorders in later centuries, is here writing about his *gens* synchronically rather than diachronically — or, if you prefer it, about the present in the past. For the past *did* matter. The history of the *gens Langobardorum* was something to boast about, marked as it was by energy, aggression (compare the destruction of the Gepids in two campaigns and a single decisive battle with the protracted Frankish campaigns against the Saxons), courage and other secular virtues.

Paul's last hero in his Lombard History is king Liutprand, who had innumerable virtues, perhaps too many to be credible: but the cultivation of letters, a care for *eruditio*, was evidently not one of them: *litterarum quidem ignarus*. By contrast, duke Arichis of Benevento and his wife were educated people, seeking out books and scholars; and by the 770s they were well ahead of the Frankish kings in that distinctively Lombard royal virtue of patronising building. Paul might well have been tempted to conclude his *Historia* with the claim that the *gens Langobardorum* lived on in Benevento, as his lord and master Arichis had recently done and as a later duke was to do more explicitly in the 860s.[53] But he was writing either in the very years in which Arichis's son and successor Grimoald was obliged to acknowledge the Frankish king's suzereinty and include his name in the dating-clauses of Beneventan documents and coins; or just after Grimoald had repudiated that subordination and the threat of reprisal was ever-present. For an Italian writer of early-Carolingian date who managed to turn the Frankish overthrow of the Lombards into a happy ending of their history — *presentem diem per [Pippini filii Karoli] adiutorium splenduit Italia, sicut fecit antiquissimis diebus* — we must go to the so-called *Historia Langobardorum codicis Gothani*.[54]

Paul, then, had written 'ethnic history' in two senses: the history of a *gens* seen in terms of its own unhappy present and the present and past of those who had deprived it of independence; and an historical narrative which gave to native oral tradition the authority of reliable testimony, comparable and even superior to other kinds of evidence. A product of the Carolingian Renaissance? If I am right, not in any legitimate use of that term. It is the case rather that the 'grammarian' Paul was one of those who provided the essential material from which Carolingian literary achievements were fashioned, just as contemporary Italian artists are now regarded — with rather less surviving evidence — as an essential precondition of Carolingian Court art.

So what becomes of Mommsen's characterisation? It must be remembered that he was writing less than a decade after the founding of the German Empire, with whose aspirations he identified himself and which could now safely absorb everything that the Classical Roman world could offer to a 'modern' society, without affecting its own essential German-ness. I suspect that he found in Paul an *Ur*-Mommsen, a 'geschichtschreibende Übermensch' combining patriotism with scholarship. We would probably be more inclined to find the type of Paul the historian in the French scholars and *lettrés* of Mommsen's generation who were not disposed to admit that Charlemagne was now 'Karl der Grosse' or that the only serious Classical scholarship was in Germany. A type and anti-type with one fundamental difference, however: the Paul of the *Historia Langobardorum* is a reminder that there need not be and was not only one contemporary view of the European eighth century, the view enunciated and disseminated by the privileged and assertive group around *Karolus rex Francorum et Langobardorum ac patricius Romanorum*.

NOTES

1. T. Mommsen, 'Die Quellen der Langobardengeschichte des Paulus Diaconus' [1880], in *Gesammelte Schriften*, 6 (Berlin 1910), pp. 485–539, the quotations from pp. 485–8.
2. D. Norberg, 'Le développement du Latin en Italie de S. Grégoire le Grand à Paul Diacre', *Settimane di Studio del Centro Italiano di Studi sull' Alto Medioevo*, 5 ii (Spoleto 1958), pp. 485–503, the quotation at p. 498. A similar view is expressed in unpublished studies of Paul's Latinity by the late Barbara Flower. For the vocabulary of the *Historia Langobardorum*, see L.J. Engels, *Observations sur le vocabulaire de Paul Diacre* (Nijmegen 1961).
3. Mommsen, 'Quellen', p. 486 n. 1, comparing H[istoria] F[rancorum] IX 25 with H[istoria] L[angobardorum] III 29. The standard edition of HL is by L. Bethmann and G. Waitz in *MGH SRL* (Hannover 1878) pp. 12–187; the standard edition of HF is by B. Krusch and W. Levison in *MGH SRM* 1 (Hannover 1951).
4. Recent summaries of the evidence are W. Levison and H. Löwe, *Deutschlands Geschichtsquellen im Mittelalter: Vorzeit u. Karolinger*, II (Weimar 1953), pp. 212–24 and H. Belting, 'Studien zum Beneventanischen Hof im 8 J.h.', *DOP* 16 (1962) pp. 164–9.
5. K. Neff, *Die Gedichte des Paulus Diaconus* (Qu. u. Untersuch. zur lat. Phil. des Mittelalters; Munich 1908), nr 1, pp. 4–6.
6. Paul's petitory poem of 782 to the Frankish king is Neff, *Gedichte*, nr 11, pp. 43–5; also in P. Godman, *Poetry of the Carolingian Renaissance* (London 1985), p. 82 with an admirable translation on p.83. The date of Paul's departure, which also has a

bearing on the date at which Charles requested and was eventually sent a copy of the Roman 'Gregorian' sacramentary, is nowhere directly recorded. But Neff, *Gedichte*, nr 23, is usually taken to mean that Paul was still in Francia in the early part of 785, although not with the king of Saxony, from which he only returned in the autumn; while *Gedichte*, nr 35, the epitaph for duke Arichis datable September 787/May 788, implies that Paul was back at Monte Cassino by that time. As Paul's letter to Adalhard of Corbie prefacing his copy of a distinctive small selection of letters of pope Gregory made in north Italy (Leningrad cod.F.v.I.7: *Codices Latini Antiquiores* ed. E.A. Lowe, 11 (Oxford 1966), nr 1603; for the area of origin see B. Bischoff, *Mittelalterliche Studien*, 3 (Stuttgart 1981) p. 30 n. 129) declares that he has been ill and without copyists from September almost to Christmas (Neff, *Gedichte*, p. 129) — in 786 rather than 785 — Hadrian's letter, Codex Carolinus nr 89 *MGH Epp* 3 p. 626, referring to Paul's conveying of the request some time previously, can hardly be earlier than the summer of 787.

7. HL I 5 with *MGH Epp* 4, pp. 507–8 and *Annales regni Francorum*, ed. F. Kurze (Hannover 1895), p. 64; HL VI 16, the *Gesta Episcoporum Mettensium* ed. G. Pertz in *MGH SS* 2, pp. 260–70.

8. HL V 6 *ad fin:* Quod nos ita factum esse probavimus, qui ante Langobardorum perditionem eandem beati Iohannis basilicam, quae utique in loco qui Modicia dicitur est constituta, per viles personas ordinari conspeximus, ita ut indignis et adulteris non pro vitae merito, sed praemiorum datione, isdem locus venerabilis largiretur.

9. Engels, *Vocabulaire*, p. 80; G. Rossetti, *Società e Istituzioni nel contado lombardo durante il Medioevo: Cologno Monzese*, 1 (Milan 1968), pp. 65 ff.

10. HL I 1, with *capit.* 1. The opening words of the text are *Septemtrionalis plaga.*

11. There are no chapter-divisions in Paul's sixteen-book *Historia Romana* (expanded from Eutropius' ten-book *Breviarium*) and *a fortiori* no chapter-titles. For important remarks on the character and significance of such titles in mss. of Augustine's works see H. Marrou, 'La division en chapitres des livres de *La Cité de Dieu*' [1951], *Patristique et Humanisme: Mélanges* (Paris 1976), pp. 253 ff. It appears that many Latin Patristic texts only acquired their *tituli* in the Carolingian period.

12. HL I 5; I. Whitaker, 'Late Classical and Early Medieval accounts of the Lapps (Sami)', *Classica et Medievalia* 34 (1983), pp. 295–7. Late nineteenth-century commentators supposed a common — lost — source for Procopius' account of the Σκριθίφινοι in *bell. Goth.* II 15 (ed. Dewing 3, p. 418), Jordanes *Getica* III 21 (ed. Mommsen, *MGH AA* 5 (1882)) in spite of the apparently erroneous name-form *Screrefennae*, and Paul; Whitaker, not unreasonably in view of Paul's phraseology here, supposes a first-hand oral account and, less plausibly, connects it with an invitation to Paul to try to convert the Danish king (cf. Neff, *Gedichte*, nr 21) — the Danes were almost as distant from the Lapps as were the Franks, and Paul denied any knowledge of their language (*Gedichte*, nr 22). The question whether *Scritofinni* was current spoken usage at the end of the eighth century is complicated rather than resolved by the Alfredian *Old-English Orosius* (ed. J.M. Bately, Early English Text Society, suppl. ser. 6, 1980) where *Scridefinne* occurs in the geographical introduction but Ohthere's account speaks of the *Finnas.*

13. Ken Gardiner, 'Paul the Deacon and Secundus of Trent' *History and Historians in Late Antiquity* ed. B. Croke, A. Emmet (Oxford 1983), p. 148.

14. HL IV 32, IV 45, VI 49.

15. The Lombard-period documents were magisterially edited by L. Schiaparelli, *Codice Diplomatico Longobardo* 1–2 (Fonti per la Storia d'Italia, Rome 1929–1933); the Frankish-period documents still have to be consulted in the edition of D. Bertini, D. Barsocchini, *Memorie e Documenti per servire all'Istoria del ducato di Lucca*, 4, 5 (Lucca 1818–44). Their importance for both regional and 'national' history may be

gathered from H. Schwarzmaier, *Lucca u. das Reich bis zum Ende des 11. Jahrhunderts* (Tübingen 1972), chs 2, 3, 5 passim. A much more profound analysis of the eighth-century evidence will, however, be found in Chris Wickham's Oxford DPhil thesis (1975), *Economy and Society in Eighth-Century North Tuscany*.

16. G.P. Bognetti, G.P. Chierici, A. de Capitani d'Arzago, *Santa Maria de Castelseprio* (Milan 1948), pp. 13–511 and in Bognetti, *L' Età Longobarda*, 2 (Milan 1966). S. Fanning, 'Lombard Arianism reconsidered', *Speculum* 56 (1981), pp. 241–58 is a sharp critique of the supposed evidence for Lombard Arianism.

17. See *PBSR*, 34 (1966), pp. 119–29.

18. Excluding, that is, tales linked with Paul's personal experiences, such as the Cunimund-skull cup (below). His most striking statement about oral material is at the end of Book I: 'Alboin's character and military victories are even now celebrated, not only among the Bavarians and the Saxons, but also among other men of the same tongue in their songs [*in eorum carminibus*]. That a superior kind of weapon [*praecipua arma*: swords?] was made in his time [*sub eo*] is related to this day by many people'. Did Paul know of the Saxon songs *before* he came to Francia? *Ignorabimus!* No trace of these northern Alboin-songs has survived: for an Old High German poem supposedly originally in Lombardic see p. 93.

19. *Origo* ed. G. Waitz, *MGH SRL* pp. 7–11; ed. B. Pagnin (Testi e Documenti medievali; Pavia s.d.).

20. H. Moisl, 'Kingship and orally transmitted *Stammestradition* among the Lombards and Franks', *Die Bayern u. ihre Nachbarn* ed. H. Wolfram, A. Schwarcz (Österr. Akad. der Wissenschaften, Ph.–hist. Kl, Denkschr 179; Vienna 1985) pp. 111–19, which reached me after the completion of this paper, draws heavily on O. Gischwantler, 'Formen langobardischer mündlicher Überlieferung', *Jahrb. f. internationale Germanistik*, 11 (1979) pp. 58–85, which I have been unable to consult.

21. J. Vansina, *Oral Tradition : a study in Historical Methodology*, Engl. transl. by H.M. Wright (London 1965); *Social Analysis* Special Issue — *Using Oral Sources: Vansina and Beyond*, ed. K. Brown and M. Roberts (Adelaide 1980), esp. the papers by J.J. Hoover and K. Brown.

22. HL IV 37: above, p. 86.

23. S. Einarsson *A History of Icelandic Literature* (Baltimore 1957), pp. 122ff, reviews previous discussions of this notion. (I am grateful to my colleague Dr. B.E. Crawford for drawing my attention to this work.) I have unfortunately been unable to consult A. Bugge, 'Paulus Diaconus' *Langobardernes Historie og dens betydning for forstaalse av anden nyere og aeldre literatur*', *Edda* 23 (1925) pp. 41–50. D. Bianchi, 'L'elemento epico nella Hist. Lang. di Paolo Diacono', *Memorie Storiche Forogiuliesi* 30 (1934), 31 (1935), 32 (1936) (!) is not helpful.

24. Vansina, *Oral Tradition*, p. 154.

25. HL IV 38; *Chronicarum Fredegarii Libri IV*, IV 69: ed. Krusch, *MGH SRM* 2 (Hannover 1888) pp. 155–6, ed. J.M. Wallace-Hadrill, *The Fourth Book of the Chronicle of Fredegar* (London-Edinburgh 1960), p. 58; T. Hodgkin, *Italy and her Invaders* 6 (Oxford 1916), pp. 59–60; Bullough in *Medium Aevum* 30 (1961) pp. 105–6. J. Jarnut, *Prosopographische u. sozialgeschtl. Studien zum Langobardenreich in Italien* (Bonn 1972) p. 371 s.n. Taso, surprisingly prefers Paul's account and dates the episode to 625 on the grounds that Gregory was exarch only in that year!

26. J.K. Bostock, *A Handbook on Old High German Literature*, 2nd ed. by K.C. King and D.R. McClintock (Oxford 1976), pp. 43–82, the quotations in the text at p.81; for a historic Lombard (but ninth-century) Hildebrand son of Eriprand see most recently Schwarzmaier, *Lucca* pp. 95ff. W. Bruckner, *Die Sprache der Langobarden* (Strasbourg 1895) pp. 18 seq and in *Zeitschr. f. deutsches Altertum* 43 (1899) pp. 47–58, attempted a partial reconstruction of the 'Lombardic epic poem' which he

believed underlay the Latin *Origo*: his efforts have subsequently been judged ingenious rather than convincing.

27. Mommsen, 'Quellen' esp. pp. 492ff; G. Waitz in *Neues Archiv* 5 (1880) pp. 417ff. Cf. K. Neff in *Neues Archiv* 17 (1892) pp. 204, E. Bernheim, *ibid.* 21 (1896) pp. 375ff, and preceding note.

28. HL I 21, referring (it is generally agreed) to the *Origo*. All three manuscript texts of the *Origo* and the unique copy of the *Historia Langobardorum codicis Gothani* (below) do in fact precede texts of the Laws, although they are all late (sc. tenth/eleventh century). For a ms. of the Edict written possibly at Pavia, before the end of the seventh century, now only known from fragments, see A. Dold, *Zur ältesten Handschrift des Edictus Rothari* (Stuttgart 1955), *CLA* 7 (Oxford 1956) nr 949, Bischoff, *Studien* 2, p. 320.

29. For the character of Secundus's work and its relationship with HL, see most recently Gardiner, 'Paul and Secundus' (n. 13 above) pp. 147–53. Bognetti's generally-thoughtful 'Processo logico e integrazione delle fonti nella storiografia di Paolo Diacono' [1951], *Età Longobarda* 3, pp. 159–84, sought to revive the discredited view that Paul's 'anecdotal' material on the early kings was already to be found in Secundus's *historiola*.

30. *Origo c. 5*; *MGH AA* 11, ed. Mommsen, p. 238 (dating the invasion to 569); *MGH AA* 9, ed. Mommsen, pp. 337–9, cf.267.

31. Aquileia-Grado: R. Cessi in *Mem. stor. Forogiul.* 25 (1929) pp. 59–66, E. Klebel in *Beiträge zur älteren europäischen Kulturgesch.: Festschrift für R. Egger*, (Klagenfurt 1952), pp. 396ff. Gardiner 'Paul and Secundus' pp. 152–3. Pavia: the fullest discussion of the late-medieval and Renaissance evidence for an earlier 'episcopal list' is that of E. Hoff, *Pavia u. seine Bischöfe im Mittelalter* (Pavia 1943) pp. 29ff; but I argued in *Atti del 4° Congresso di Studi sull'Alto Medioevo* (Spoleto 1969) pp. 317ff that this requires substantial revision (a preliminary presentation only — but the intended fuller discussion of the evidence is now unlikely to be written). Of the (?) 13 seventh/eighth-century bishops in the 'lists' (Hoff pp. 3–4, *Atti 4° Congr.* p. 320), Paul names only three — Anastasius, Damian and Peter (I).

32. *MGH Leges* 4 (1868) ed. F. Bluhme, pp. 2–3; F. Beyerle (ed.) *Die Gesetze der Langobarden* (Weimar 1947), pp. 2–4.

33. HL VI 52 (the earliest reference to *Carniola*, Krain); id.56; HL II 28. If 'oral tradition' correctly reported Aistulf's heroic deed *in quodam ponte* in the wooded area between Fano and Fossombrone (VI 56), the most plausible site is where the Ponte S. Cipriano (of 1611 — apparently eliminating all traces of a Roman bridge: cf. M.H. Ballance, 'The Roman bridges of the Via Flaminia', *PBSR* 19 (1951) pp. 78ff) carries the Flaminia across the Rio Maggiore.

34. HL VI 1; Belting in *DOP* 16, pp. 164ff; N. Acocella, 'Le origini della Salerno medievale negli scritti di Paolo Diacono', *Rivista di Studi Salernitani* 1 (1968) pp. 23–64.

35. HL I 23, 24; HR XVI 20 (ed. Crivellucci p. 236); Jordanes ed. Mommsen, *MGH AA*, 5 pp. 52 (*Romana*), 83, 109ff, 125ff, 135 (*Getica*); Procopius, *History of the Wars* VIII 18: ed. H.B. Dewing (1928) pp. 234 seq.

36. Einarsson, pp. 12, 126–7, cf.114.

37. HL II 14–22, on which see R. Thomsen, *The Italic Regions* (Copènhagen 1948), pp. 252–60.

38. Acocella (n. 34) p. 60 translates as 'i libri degli antenati'. Perhaps.

39. *MGH Epp* 4, pp. 507–8; P. Godman, *Poetry* (n. 6 above) pp. 9–10, 86 seq.

40. *Gesta* in *MGH SS* 2, p. 264, reporting a folkloric tale about Arnulf and a lost ring from Charles's own mouth.

41. Neff, *Gedichte* nr 34. But if the attribution to Alcuin (on stylistic grounds) is accepted, the poem must necessarily be dated 794–6.

42. HL II 2, III 9, 17, 22, 29 (cf. 43), 31 etc.
43. HL VI 16, I 5.
44. For Paul's use of Gregory see Waitz's notes to his edition of HL, Mommsen 'Quellen' p. 486 n. 1 (comparing HF IX 25 with HL III 29), Bognetti 'Processo' (n. 29) pp. 161ff. Note that HF was already used in the composition of the Gesta episcoporum Mettensium: Krusch-Levison in MGH SRM 1/1 (ed. 2), p. xxiii.
45. Chronica monasterii Casinensis, ed. H. Hoffmann, MGH SS 34; Krusch-Levison pp. xxiii–xxv; E.A. Lowe (Loew), The Beneventan Script (Oxford 1914/Rome 1980) p. 309.
46. Crivellucci, ed.cit., p. xxxviii and pp. 184–8, with the unlikely claim (187 n.) that the source of Paul's dum Aetius minime annuisset, eo quod contra viciniores hostes occupatus existeret is HE I 13: utpote qui [sc. Aetius] gravissimis eo tempore bellis cum Blaedla et Attila regibus Hunnorum erat occupatus.
47. HE V 7, with (I.9 of the epitaph) redivivae where Paul has recidivae (no variant readings reported). For the Court hand in Cambridge Univ. Libr. Ms. Kk. V. 16 fol. 128ᵛ, see P.H. Blair, R.A.B. Mynors, The Moore Bede (Early Engl Mss in Facsimile 9, 1959), B. Bischoff, 'Die Hofbibliothek Karls der Grossen' [1965], Studien 3, pp. 160–1.
48. Gregory Registrum IX 67 and IX 66 (MGH Epp 2, ed. Ewald and Hartmann, pp. 87–8, 86) in HL IV 9, idem IX 126 (Epp 2, p. 127) in HL IV 19: otherwise only in the 'C' collection, transmitted by the three ninth-century mss. Cologne Diözesanbibl. cod 92 (Cologne, s IX¹), Vatican ms Pal Lat 266 (W. Germany, s IX¹), Düsseldorf Univ. bibl. cod B 79 (N.W. Germany). For Paul's copy of the 'P' collection, see above, n. 6.
49. HL I 2, I 15; L.D. Reynolds (ed.), Texts and Transmission: [a survey of the Latin Classics] (Oxford 1983), pp. 307–12 (where Alcuin's reference to but not Paul's use of the Natural History is noted). R.H. Rouse, Texts and Transmission p. 157 unexpectedly credits the single citation of Donatus gramaticus in expositione Vergilii (HL II 23) to Ti. Claudius Donatus, which if correct suggests that his Interpretationes Vergilianae were also read by Paul in Francia (cf id. pp. 157–8).
50. Getica 1, MGH AA 5 p. 53.
51. HL I 1–2, 4–6; HE I 1 (for the sources see Plummer's edition, Oxford 1896, pp. 9ff); HF I 1–23 (the Resurrection), followed by chapters on the Apostolic and sub-Apostolic ages and the Persecutions; HF II 9; Fredegarius in MGH SRM 2, ed. Krusch (1888) pp. 45–6, 93. Paul was evidently aware of the Frankish Troy-legend: see Gesta, MGH SS 2, p. 264.
52. HL I 13; id.I 23. With the first of these compare Edictus Rothari c. 224: de manomissionibus (MGH Leges, 4, pp. 54–5, Gesetze ed. Beyerle p. 88) where in gaida et gisil is now generally recognised as the Langobardic 'original' of Paul's per sagittam: Gesetze pp. 502, 503; F. van der Rhee, Die germanischen Wörter in den langobardischen Gesetzen (Rotterdam 1970), pp. 66–7.
53. HL VI 58; Belting 'Studien' (n. 4) pp. 169ff, Acocella (n. 34); Belting 'Studien' pp. 149ff; MGH Leges 4, p. 210, Gesetze, pp. 392–4.
54. P. Grierson in Karl der Grosse: Lebenswerk und Nachleben, ed. W. Braunfels, 1 (Düsseldorf 1965), p. 516; O. Bertolini, ibid., pp. 656–8; MGH SRL p. 11, whose anonymous author's non-use of HL (long commented on) presents no problem if my reading of Paul's text is substantially correct!

VII

ROMANITAS AND CAMPANILISMO: AGNELLUS OF RAVENNA'S VIEW OF THE PAST

T.S. Brown

Andreas Agnellus, abbot and deacon of Ravenna, has long been one of the least known and least studied of early medieval writers. Although there has been a flickering of interest in his work in recent years, its significance has often been misunderstood. For example, Chris Wickham described him in his excellent history of early medieval Italy as 'a competent chronicler', and as 'the best historian in Italy' along with Erchempert of Capua.[1] Neither description is justified. Partly this is because his powers of analysis and coherent narrative are woefully inadequate. His chronology is always vague and often hopelessly muddled, and his handling of written sources is uncritical, although he does make important use of local consular annals. These are weaknesses which he shares with all but a handful of early medieval historians. Strictly, however, his work belongs not to the genre of history but to that of episcopal biography. His work is entitled the *Liber Pontificalis Ecclesiae Ravennatis*, and is loosely modelled on the Roman *Liber Pontificalis*, although the Ravenna work was written by a single author while the Roman archetype was built up gradually by a succession of biographers. From the late eighth-century the prestige of the papal *Liber* started a fashion for biographical studies of important sees (and monasteries), of which the best known example is Paul the Deacon's *History of the Bishops of Metz*.[2] Within this proliferating genre Agnellus' work is a very distinctive specimen; it did not attract a continuator, it had no apparent impact outside Ravenna and it is highly idiosyncratic in approach.[3]

Only in a very loose sense can Agnellus' work be described as a history of the see of Ravenna, and its contents are rarely historical. His perspective is partly that of the anecdotal raconteur, partly that of the antiquarian who lovingly collects inscriptions and describes monuments, but predominantly that of an opinionated cleric, eager to put across his narrow but strongly held views of religious rectitude and to bring in his own contemporary prejudices at every turn. These include virulent dislike of Franks, Greeks, popes and, perhaps surprisingly, most bishops of his own see, whom he denounced as 'ravenous beasts' intent on depriving their clergy of its legitimate rights.[4] Much of the work is tediously homiletic, thanks to its moralising injunctions, its long biblical quotations, and its remarkably oratorical, even hectoring, tone. It was in fact delivered in the form of lectures to interested clergy and laity of Ravenna and then copied down verbatim. This is clear from remarks made by the author, such as 'The sun lengthens the shadows and the day grows dark', 'yesterday, constrained by a slight physical indisposition, I was unable to narrate all the marvels of this saintly man' and 'let this suffice for today; the time is come for us to return indoors'.[5]

Since Agnellus was immersed in the activities and concerns of a churchman, it is hardly surprising that his is predominantly a work of religious culture rather than of secular history, with elements of hagiography, liturgy, exegesis and devotional poetry prominent throughout. His historical assumptions are limited and conventional, centred on a providential view of God's intervention in human affairs and a pessimistic preoccupation with the impending end of the world.[6] For these reasons Agnellus' work does not fit into an easily defined category; it is a confused, exasperating pot-pourri of a work. But for the modern reader this is precisely the merit of Agnellus; in his discursive, partisan way he always wears his heart on his sleeve, and so reveals his preoccupations with a vividness and fullness which a more deliberate historian could never match. He also presents us with fascinating evidence of oral traditions, which may well have played a role in a post-Roman clerical environment not dissimilar from that played in Lombard society by the traditions preserved by Paul the Deacon.[7] It is curious that his data on contemporary *mentalités* has hardly been tapped; only very desultory use has been made of Agnellus as a political source for Late Roman and Byzantine Italy, and by far the greatest attention has been paid to his descriptions of buildings and mosaics, which are, of course, extremely detailed and valuable.[8]

Only the bare outline of Agnellus' life can be reconstructed. He was born around 800 into one of the most influential aristocratic families of Ravenna. He held the office of deacon within the cathedral church of his city, drew income from two churches of which he was 'abbot' by hereditary right, and may have held some official post in charge of the see's buildings. His 'book' was delivered in lecture form over a number of years from about 832 onwards. The author does not appear to have travelled widely away from Ravenna, although he did attend the baptism of the emperor Lothar I's daughter at Pavia. He possessed a passionate devotion to the rights and wealth of his see, which is reflected in his staunch defence of Ravenna's jurisdictional claims and his bitter resentment of papal authority over Ravenna in both the ecclesiastical and political spheres.[9]

The areas of early medieval life on which Agnellus throws light are legion. Numerous passages, for example, highlight the material concerns of the contemporary secular clergy. These clerics mouthed watchwords about simony and moral laxity which anticipate those of tenth- and eleventh-century reformers, while displaying a fascination with lay and ecclesiastical wealth and a preoccupation with their own privileges and incomes. Agnellus defended his colleagues' rights with the energy of an ecclesiastical shop-steward, and even records with approval a clerical 'strike' against Archbishop Theodore, which was only resolved by the intervention of the exarch as arbitrator.[10]

Of particular interest is Agnellus' view of the Roman past and his attitude to the Ravenna of his own day. One would expect such a writer to feel a close sense of identity with the Roman world. Ravenna was a city which had played an enormously important role in the Late Roman and Byzantine periods, and where the degree of physical and institutional continuity was unmatched in all Italy. In fact his attitude was surprisingly ambiguous. He attested the survival of quintessentially Roman activities such as public games and bathing, and he described Ravenna proudly as 'a second Rome'.[11] He went to excessive lengths in his emulation of Virgil and of the Christian poets of the Late Empire.[12] But he had no time whatsoever for the Byzantines, whom he denounced as *Graeci* and even as 'serpents'; significantly he only referred to them as *Romani* when he was quoting from another source.[13] But for all his pessimism about the present he had little nostalgia for or particular interest in the old Roman empire; he was always eager to pass on to a trivialising anecdote, to describe the physical magnificence of monuments or to score rather petty points. For example, the attribution of a statue to the emperor Zeno became the pretext for a digression which explained his proficiency as a runner by his lack of kneecaps.[14] Agnellus took the Roman empire very much for granted, and indeed for him the empire still existed. For all the plagues, famines, floods and *vexationes gentium* that crowd his pages, there is no sense of a break with the past, and he could easily relate to Roman traditions at least on the level of individual figures and anecdotes. The Franks were cordially disliked (especially for despoiling Ravenna of its treasures), and Charlemagne was accused of caesaropapist pretensions through the medium of an amusing story in which a seemingly simple archbishop called him 'papa' at the dinner table.[15] But it is striking that the legitimacy of Charles's title as Roman emperor is never questioned. The ideology of the Donation of Constantine had triumphed in Ravenna, and even such a marked anti-papalist as Agnellus accepted that the right to crown emperors was vested in the pope.[16] Agnellus' grudging respect for Rome is based not on its classical past but on its position as the see of St Peter, and the great lengths to which he went to elevate the legendary St Apollinaris into a companion of St Peter was a tribute to the papacy's prestige.[17]

How can Agnellus' lack of enthusiasm for the Roman world be explained? Pragmatic realism, sheer petty-mindedness and a characteristically medieval failure to grasp the distinctiveness of the past all perhaps played their part. Most important of all, his attention was always focused on his own city, Ravenna, and its relations with powerful outside forces are seen as essentially passive: Ravenna was seen as the recipient of favours from old (i.e. good) emperors and of ill treatment from new (i.e. bad) rulers and popes. What mattered to Agnellus was not any positive contribution or commitment to the Roman world, but the spiritual and material welfare of his own more cohesive community, a city with its traditions, rights and of course saints and their relics.

Agnellus' horizons are remarkably limited even by early medieval standards. In a bizarre distortion of one source (Paul the Deacon) he portrayed the Blue and Green factions as devastating Egypt and Syria and plundering the True Cross, when the real culprits were the Persians. The explanation may lie in the fact that factional strife was something which he was very familiar with from Ravenna, and very concerned about.[18] The question then arises of whether this local consciousness or parochialism was a recent development in Agnellus' time, or whether it had its roots earlier in the Roman period. Whatever one's views on the strength of local community feeling in the Roman world, it is worth stressing how cosmopolitan and rootless the society of Ravenna was in the fifth and sixth centuries; all new capitals, like Brasilia and Canberra today, are cities of immigrants. But in the few early works that survive, such as the sermons of Peter Chrysologus and the Passion of St Apollinaris, which probably goes back to the sixth century, the sense of local pride emerges very strongly. The formative, unifying influences on a community of this sort were ecclesiastical — the growth of local cults, the growing power and authority of the bishop with his duties to the local *populus*, and an increasing preoccupation with salvation, which can only have weakened secular ties and ambition within a wider Roman state and society.[19]

This heightened sense of local community and narrowing of perspectives seem very largely to have been the product of increasing spiritual preoccupations and ecclesiastical authority. Agnellus vividly reflects these developments, since in his eyes the patron saint and his earthly representative, the bishop, formed the focus of local pride and allegiance. It is hardly surprising that two of the most telling tributes to eighth-century civic pride, the verses in praise of Milan and Verona, stem from a clerical milieu comparable with that of Agnellus.[20] Of course Agnellus' loyalties lay predominantly with the clerical establishment, which displayed a quite remarkable corporate spirit. The city's patron was seen as the defender of the clergy's interests to the extent that discontented clerics called upon Apollinaris personally to 'save us' and to 'fight for us'.[21] The hatred of Agnellus and his colleagues for their great rival, the see of Rome, exceeded the antipathies of the most partisan football fan. Instructive here is his regret at Archbishop Maximian's failure to obtain the relics of St Andrew from Justinian. Agnellus commented:

> And indeed, brothers, if the body of the blessed Andrew, brother of Peter, prince of the apostles, had been buried here, the Roman pontiffs would not have subjugated us at all like this.[22]

This local pride was not however confined to the clergy. Agnellus' text demonstrates that it had also taken root among the lay population. The author had close links of kinship and friendship with the local secular aristocracy, whose way of life and concerns he shared. Like his near contemporary Notker of St Gall he bitterly denounced episcopal vice and venality, but unlike Notker the monk he abhorred secular ills such as factional violence and official corruption in a very immediate and concerned way. He took a close interest in the political, economic and military life of his city, and he was proud that his archbishop was ruling Romagna just like an exarch and 'arranged everything as the Romans were accustomed to do'.[23] The figures of the past portrayed as contributing to Ravenna's greatness are not just churchmen but lay men and women such as Julianus Argentarius and Galla Placidia. Agnellus prided himself on the fact that one of his lay ancestors rallied the whole population, including clergy, into a militia to resist a punitive force sent out by his *bête noir*, the emperor Justinian II.[24]

It can therefore be seen that, while Agnellus' work is *not* a chronicle, it forms an excellent guide to the resilience of urban life and the nature of civic consciousness in early medieval Ravenna. A large measure of continuity with the Roman past is still taken for granted, and here Agnellus' views contrast with those of Carolingian historians in the North, whose writings reflect a disjunction with the classical past.[25] His work also has many of the features of the later Italian civic chronicle; admittedly Agnellus was a spokesman for the clergy, but then the ecclesiastical elite dominated the administration of the city in a manner analogous to that of the later *comune*, and civic patriotism was still seen in a largely ecclesiastical light. For all its shortcomings as history, the long-neglected work of Agnellus stands out as an unparalleled guide not only to the past of a great Roman city but also to the rise of a new, narrowly focused local pride or *campanilismo*. It is appropriate that the bell-towers which have given their name to this distinctly Italian concept first appeared in Ravenna during the century in which Agnellus composed his work.[26]

NOTES

1. C. Wickham, *Early Medieval Italy* (London, 1981), 29, 147.
2. On the Roman *Liber Pontificalis* and its influence *La Storiografia Altomedievale (Setti-mane di Studio del Centro Italiano di Studi sull'Alto Medioevo)*, xvii (1970), is fundamental, particularly the paper by O. Bertolini.
3. See G. Fasoli, 'Rileggendo il *"Liber Pontificalis"* di Agnello Ravennate', *Spoleto*, xvii, 457–95 and the published discussion. Significantly, Agnellus' work survives in only one complete ms. (Modena, Bibl. Estense, X, p. 49, 15th cent.) and was not published until 1708 (by B. Bacchini). Medieval and modern interest in Agnellus is assessed by O. Capitani, 'Agnello Ravennate nella recente storia della storiografia medioevale', *Felix Ravenna*, v–vi (1973), 183–98, and A. Vasina, *Lineamenti culturali dell'Emilia-Romagna* (Ravenna, 1978), 79–148.
4. A typical example occurs in *c.* 118, ed. O. Holder-Egger, *MGH, SRL*, 356: *iste in sua sede ut lupus in grege, leo inter quadrupedia, geracis inter volatilia, procella in maturis fructibus* (he [Archbishop Theodore] behaved towards his see as a wolf among sheep, a lion among cattle, a hawk among birds, a storm in the midst of ripe crops). The partial edition by A. Testi Rasponsi, *Codex Pontificalis Ecclesie Ravennatis*, Muratori, new ed., ii, iii, i (Bologna, 1922) offers a superior version of the text up to *c.* 104, but the references given here are to the *MGH* edition throughout, partly for the sake of consistency and partly because it is more widely accessible.
5. *C. 38, SRL*, 302: *iamque sol duplicat unbras et obtenebrescit dies:c.* 39, *ibid.*, *esterna denique die modica molestia corporis coartatus, non vobis omnia valui praedicti sancti viri miracula narrare*; *c.* 62, *SRL*, 322: *sufficiat nunc ista hodie, tempus est iam in aede revertamur*. On the manner in which Agnellus composed his work, see A. Testi Rasponi, 'Note marginali al *"Liber Pontificalis"* di Agnello Ravennate', *Atti e Memorie della Reale Deputazione di storia Patria per la Romagna*, 3ª ser, xxvii (1897), 86–134, 4ª ser, i (1909–1910), 224–346. The language of Agnellus, which oscillates wildly from the colloquial to the impenetrably pompous, ought to be of the greatest interest to philologists.
6. The religious elements in Agnellus' work are stressed by G. Cortesi, 'Andrea Agnello e il *"Liber Pontificalis Ecclesiae Ravennatis"*, *Corsi di Cultura sull' Arte Ravennate e Bizantina*, xxviii (1981), 31–76.
7. *Cf.* D. Bullough, 'Ethnic history? Paul the Deacon's *Historia Langobardorum*, *supra*, 91–93. However the notion advanced by N. Tamassia and V. Ussani, 'Epica e storia in alcuni capitoli di Agnello Ravennate', *Nuovi Studi Medievali*, i (1923), 14–31, that passages of Agnellus were derived from a civic verse epic, strikes the present writer as far-fetched.
8. Works employing Agnellus' art-historical data include H.L. Gonin, *Excerpta Agnelliana* (Utrecht, 1933), A.W. Byvanck, 'De mozaiken te Ravenna het *Liber Pontificalis Ecclesiae Ravennatis*', *Mededeelingen van het Nederlandsch Historisch*

Instituut te Rome, viii (1928), 61–82, and F.W. Deichmann's magisterial *Ravenna, Hauptstadt des spätantiken Abendlandes* (Wiesbaden, 1966–1974). For historical use of Agnellus see T.S. Brown, 'La chiesa di Ravenna durante il regno di Giustiniano', *Corsi di Cultura sull'Arte Ravennate e Bizantina*, xxx (1983), 266–90, *idem, Gentlemen and Officers. Imperial Administration and Aristocratic Power in Byzantine Italy* A.D. 554–800 (London, 1984), and G. Fasoli, 'Il dominio territoriale degli arcivescovi di Ravenna fra l'VIII e l'XI secolo', in *I poteri temporali dei vescovi in Italia e in Germania nel medioevo*, ed. C–G. Mor and H. Schmiedingen (Bologna, 1979), 87–140, who lists *ibid.*, 92, n. 34, the most important recent work on Agnellus.

9. On Agnellus' life see Fasoli, 'Rileggendo', 463–5, Cortesi, 'Andrea Agnello', 33–41 and Testi Rasponi, 'Note'. Visit to Pavia: *c.* 171, *SRL*, 388. On Ravenna's rivalry with Rome see T.S. Brown, 'The imperial administration and the church of Ravenna in the seventh-century', *EHR*, xciv (1979), 1–28.

10. Cc. 121–3, *SRL*, 358–9. The conflicting attitudes to reform in tenth- and eleventh-century Ravenna are reflected in the careers of two of the city's native sons, St Romuald and St Peter Damian.

11. C. 128, SRL, 62: *clausa sunt balnea, cessaverunt spectacula publica* (the baths were closed, the public games were cancelled). An example of Agnellus' pride in his city as a *secular* rival to Rome occurs in *c.* 40, *SRL*, 305:*iussit atque decrevit, ut absque Roma Ravenna esset caput Italiae* (He [Valentinian III] commanded and decreed that apart from Rome Ravenna should be the capital of Italy), In *c.* 94, *SRL*, 338, a mosaic portrait of Theodoric is described as accompanied by parallel depictions of Rome and Ravenna.

12. Virgil is warmly praised in *c.* 166, *SRL*, 384. On one passage modelled on a line of the *Aeneid* see Brown, *Gentlemen*, 98, n. 34.

13. Greeks as *serpentes*: *c.* 140, *SRL*, 369. Cf. W. Ohnsorge, 'L'idea d'imperio nel secolo nono e l'Italia meridionale', *Atti del 3° Congresso Internazionale di Studi sull'Alto-Medioevo* (Spoleto, 1959), 261–2.

14. C. 94, SRL, 338: *Alii aiunt, quod supradictus equus pro amore Zenonis imperatoris factus fuisset ... pro nimia velocitate pedum eum Leo imperator generum sumpsit ... Hic vero patellis genuculorum non habuit, et sic currebat fortiter, ut arrepto cursu quadrigas pedibus iungeret* (Some say that this horse had been made in honour of the emperor Zeno ... he was accepted as son-in-law by the emperor Leo on account of his extraordinary fleetness of foot. This man had no knee-caps, which enabled him to run so strongly that, when he ran, he could catch up with a chariot). The story is inaccurately taken from the Anonymus Valesianus.

15. C. 165, SRL, 383–4 and *cf.* Ohnsorge, *loc. cit.* The story is based on a pun involving the words *papa* ('pope') and *pappa* ('munch' or 'eat up').

16. C. 94, SRL, 338: *Karolus rex Francorum ... Romanorum percepisset a Leo papa imperium* (Charles, king of the Franks, received the office of Roman emperor from Pope Leo III).

17. *Cf.* Brown, 'La chiesa', and *idem*, 'The imperial administration'.

18. C. 107, SRL, 348, a garbled version of *Historia Langobardorum*, iv. 36. Agnellus' abhorrence of factional disorder is most evident in cc. 127–8, *SRL*, 361–2.

19. Cf. Brown *Gentlemen*, 157–8 and 175–89; A.M. Orselli, 'Il santo patrono cittadino: genesi e sviluppo del patrocinio del vescovo nei secoli VI e VII', in S. Boesch Gajano, ed., *Agiografia Altomedievale* (Bologna, 1976), 85–104.

20. On the *Versus de Mediolano* and *Versus de Verona* see J.K. Hyde, 'Medieval descriptions of cities', *BJRL*, xlviii (1966), 311–13.

21. *c.* 122, *SRL*, 358: *salva nos...certa pro nobis.*

22. C. 76, SRL, 329: *Et re vera, fratres, quia, si corpus beati Andreae, germani Petri principis, hic humasset, nequaquam nos Romani pontifices sic subiugasset.*

23. On the ties of Agnellus with the laity see Brown, *Gentlemen*, 170–2, 180. C. 159, *SRL*, 380: *iudicavit iste...totum Pentapolim veluti exarchus* (he [Archbishop Sergius] ruled all of the Pentapolis just like an exarch), *sic omnia disponebat, ut soliti sunt modo Romani facere*.

24. C. 140, *SRL*, 369–70.

25. J. Moorhead, 'The West and the Roman past from Theodoric to Charlemagne', in B. Croke and A.M. Emmett, eds., *History and Historians in Late Antiquity* (Sydney, 1983), 163.

26. K. Conant, *Carolingian and Romanesque Architecture* (2nd rev.ed., Harmondsworth, 1978), 104–5. An annotated translation of Agnellus' work has been undertaken by the Medieval Source Workshop of Edinburgh University and should be published in the near future.

IX

ASSER'S *LIFE OF ALFRED*

James Campbell

Asser, a Welsh cleric, entered the service of King Alfred in about 886. Seven years later he wrote a life of his lord, most unusual in being written during the lifetime of its subject; for Alfred did not die until 899.[1] Its plan is curious: after its introductory account of Alfred's birth and descent, it can be divided into six sections: three are annalistic, describing events, most military, and largely derived from an early version of the *Anglo-Saxon Chronicle*; these alternate with three sections describing aspects of the king's life and character. The book is sometimes rambling and disjointed, with inconsequential and apparently contradictory elements, even at crucial points, and is written in a style in which eloquence vies with clumsiness. The loose construction has suggested, though it does not prove, that our text is a draft.[2] Some of what Asser says, and the way in which he says it, falls oddly on the ears of historians more accustomed to medieval centuries other than the ninth. For example V.H. Galbraith wrote of Asser's lacking 'the humour and the immediacy which belong to contemporary writing' and felt an instinctive distrust which helped him to the conviction that the work is a fake.[3] It is not a fake; and it is very important.[4] The only known life of an English king written before the eleventh century, it has to be considered beside the other works composed at Alfred's court: the *Chronicle*, the *Laws*, and the translation of Latin works of edification. The 'Alfredian Renaissance' is a singular phenomenon in the history of learning, and of the state. Fully to understand the nature and origins of Asser's work would be to understand much else about the relationships between learning and power in Dark Age Europe. I say 'would be', not 'is', because as far as I am concerned, the nature of the book is by no means fully understood.

One thing of which one can be reasonably sure is that Asser's work stands in a Carolingian historical tradition. The relationship between Wessex and the Carolingians was a substantial one. Alfred's grandfather, Egbert, had been an exile at Charlemagne's court at a time when its leading intellectual was the English Alcuin. Alfred's stepmother (later sister-in-law), Judith, was a Carolingian princess. Very prominent among the scholars whom Alfred took into his service were Grimbald of St Bertin's, sent with the aid of Fulk, archbishop of Rheims, and John the

Old Saxon, who, as abbot of Alfred's new monastery at Athelney, had many Franks in his community (two of whom tried to murder him).[5] There were other well-known links. Similarities between the intellectual activities at the Carolingian court and those at that of Alfred are evident. For example, the Anglo-Saxon Chronicle, composed *c.* 892, is a counterpart to the Frankish royal annals, composed *c.* 780 (and reveals a strong interest in Carolingian affairs). The intellectual life at Alfred's court has significant similarities to that at Charlemagne's.[6] Such resemblances cannot be pressed too far. There was a vast difference in the scale of intellectual activity. Compare the amount of Carolingian verse surviving in Latin, six thick quarto *Monumenta* volumes, with what we have of what is known for certain to have been written in England in the century after Alfred's accession, a few score lines at most.[7] The differences between the execution of the English *Chronicle* and the Frankish annals are as striking as the similarities in their overall design.[8] Nevertheless, the case for seeking a context for Asser's work in Francia is strong, and the stronger in that his vocabulary shows Frankish influence. (He may have studied in Gaul, but this cannot be proved.[9])

One link between Asser and Carolingian royal biography is indisputable. He had read Einhard's preface.[10] Galbraith maintained that he 'drew his inspiration' from Einhard, and Beryl Smalley suggested that 'Asser did his utmost to fit the story of Alfred into Einhard's pattern', though adding 'but he did not succeed'.[11] If Asser seeks to follow Einhard he is in a firmly classical tradition, for no other medieval author is so close to a classical model as is Einhard to Suetonius. It was not unjustly that Halphen said that the *Life of Charlemagne* 'apparaît souvent plus comme la treizième "vie des Césars" que comme une œuvre originale'.[12] Einhard's highly controlled treatment of his subject is the Suetonian one, 'neque per tempora sed per species'.[13] The influence of his model is apparent at every turn. Einhard was the disciple of Suetonius; was Asser the disciple of Einhard?

To some extent, he was. He seems conscious of Einhard as a model when he draws on Einhard's preface just at one of the points at which he turns from annalistic narrative to a passage of personal description. In such passages he selects such themes as Einhard and Suetonius select: Alfred's interest in the liberal arts, his building works, his generosity to strangers. In addition, one long passage may derive from Einhard, though Einhard has nothing directly corresponding to it. This is Asser's account of how Alfred divided up his income, allocating it in allegedly precise fractions to various secular and religious purposes.[14] The *descriptio atque divisio* of Charlemagne's goods, which Einhard quotes *in toto*, makes similarly precise allocations.[15] It may be that Asser's description of the division of Alfred's income, unparalleled, I believe,

elsewhere, is an attempt to do for him what Einhard's inclusion of the
descriptio atque divisio did for Charlemagne: giving more than rhetorical
definition to the scale of his pious generosity.[16]

Nevertheless, there are many differences between Asser and Einhard.
Most blatant is this: over half of Asser's book consists of annals directly
derived from the *Chronicle*. They cover not only Alfred's reign up to 887,
but also the years from his birth to his accession; these earlier annals
being linked to a biographical purpose by the inclusion of dates in terms
of Alfred's age. Einhard's approach is strictly, very strictly, non-
annalistic. Asser's annals fill his work with *Anno Domini* dates; the *Vita
Caroli* includes only one such, and that is in Charlemagne's *descriptio
atque divisio*, copied — not composed — by Einhard.[17] In his annalistic
sections Asser differs from Einhard not only in the mode in which he
presents information but in the kind of information he presents. Thus,
while Asser describes many military incidents, Einhard is concerned to
tell of 'vitae illius modum potius quam bellorum quae gessit eventus';[18]
and, although he provides succinct summaries of campaigns, the only
military *eventus* of which he gives much detail is Roncevaux. Asser's
annals say something of deeds of men who were not royal: Einhard does
not name any Frank outside the royal family, apart from five noblemen;
all of whom appear only on being slain in battle.[19] Asser says something
of Alfred's childhood; Einhard nothing of Charlemagne's. In his
non-annalistic passages, those most important ones describing the
character and conduct of the king, Asser, like Einhard, eschews A.D.
dates. But even in those passages he differs from Einhard in style, and in
more than style. There is no direct speech in Einhard, much in Asser.
Einhard uses the first person only in his preface, and it is by one general
sentence there that he establishes himself as an intimate of Charlemagne
and as eyewitness (no doubt in part to meet the Isidorean requirements
that a historian should have seen, or heard directly of, what he describes).
Asser's work is in part autobiographical; references to himself, often as a
witness, are many. Differences in vocabulary between the two authors
are more than superficially significant. Consider a word which Einhard
uses and Asser does not: *fortuna*; and one which Asser uses and Einhard
does not: *Christus*. Asser cites the Bible often, Einhard never. Einhard
follows Suetonius in saying something of the sexual life of his hero, and
in occasionally verging upon criticism. True, he does not follow him far
in either direction; but there is nothing at all to correspond in Asser.

Other Carolingian biographies can be set beside Asser's: in particular
the lives of Louis the Pious by Thegan (written c. 837) and by the
anonymous 'Astronomer' (written not long after the emperor's death in
840).[20] Similarities between, in particular, Thegan's book and Asser's
have been well brought out by Professor Bullough: both authors are

writing in their subject's lifetime; both begin with a royal genealogy; both have a basically annalistic structure.[21] Thegan is unlike Asser in that he makes hardly any use of direct speech. The Astronomer, on the other hand, does use direct speech, though not to the extent that Asser does. Both he and Thegan, like Asser and unlike Einhard, make extensive use of the Bible. The Astronomer presents Louis as a ruler of intense personal piety, as Asser does Alfred. (It is true that some of the resemblances between these authors and Asser may be due to similarities in the circumstances they describe: thus both Asser and Thegan emphasis the superiority of a youngest son to his brothers; but then, both Alfred and Louis *were* youngest sons.)

In important ways the works of the biographers of Louis the Pious fit with Asser's. It cannot be proved that he knew them; but at the very least he was grappling with the same problems as his Carolingian counterparts of two generations before: in such a way that the similarities and dissimilarities between his work and theirs deserve serious consideration.

This is particularly so in respect of the annalistic element. Preponderant in Asser, it is overwhelmingly dominant in Thegan and the Astronomer. Walafrid Strabo described Thegan's work as *opusculum in morem annalium*, and such it is.[22] After a brief account of the origins of the Carolingian dynasty, and of Louis's life up to the death of Charlemagne, Thegan begins to describe events year by year, and sticks consistently to the annalistic mode thereafter. There are two excursuses: having described the coronation of Louis by Pope Stephen, Thegan gives a longish description of the appearance, dress and characteristics of Louis; the rebellion of 833 provides the opportunity for a long diatribe against low-born bishops.[23] Similarly with the Astronomer. He begins with an outline of the reign of Charlemagne and an account of Louis's birth. Thereafter his long book (nearly twice as long as Asser's) is strictly annalistic: on occasion, but rarely, there is something like an excursus: on the siege of Barcelona; on a story about a raid on the Spanish march; above all on Louis's pious character, as shown in particular by his rule in Aquitaine.[24] These authors are even more annalistic in their approach than is Asser; yet in a very important respect they depart from annalistic conventions as he does not: they are singularly sparing with A.D. dates. The Astronomer gives such dates only for the birth of Louis and for the death of Charlemagne.[25] Thegan gives one one A.D. date only.[26] Both authors were drawing heavily on annalistic sources which had dates. Yet they leave them out, and were it not for the helpfulness of modern editors in inserting dates in the margin, they would leave the reader struggling from unnumbered year to unnumbered year. The one date which Thegan gives suggests awareness of the problems he was causing. It comes in his first sentence, which simply says in what year his work begins: 'Regnante domino nostro Iesu Christo in perpetuum. Anno incarnationis eius octingentesimo tredecimo, qui est annus regni gloriosi et orthodoxi imperatoris Karoli quadragesimus quintus.[27] It provides a key to the establishment of approximate A.D. dates for the rest of the book; and perhaps that is why it was given.

The role of annalistic material in Asser, Thegan and the Astronomer indicates something of the predicament of would-be royal biographers in the ninth century. A need was felt for works which combined biographical treatment in a style owing something to Suetonius, with the kind of information provided by annals. Two genres, hitherto largely distinct, are brought together. Speaking of classical, and by implication medieval, historians in general Beryl Smalley said 'No author would have thought of composing a *Life and Times* of his subject: that would have meant mixing two separate genres'.[28] But that is just what these authors are doing. One may ask: why should they have bothered? Why not produce brief biographical sketches to set beside annals rather than attempt, very imperfectly, to turn annals into a biography? I do not know; but the wish to produce a work *combining* the two genres also appears in a composite work, found in a ninth-century manuscript in which chapters of Einhard's *Vita* are inserted into the *Annales Regni Francorum*. 'Finiunt gesta domni Caroli', says the manuscript after recording the death of Charlemagne, 'Incipit vita eiusdem principis', then, having given sixteen chapters of Einhard, it goes on (after a blank page) 'Incipit gesta Hludowici'.[29] That Asser was not alone in the ninth-century in feeling the need to combine annals and biography gives more interest to the way in which he does it. His retention of the dates from the annals he incorporates can be seen as sensible. The one A.D. date which he provides, which is not derived from the *Anglo-Saxon Chronicle*, appears in the first sentence of his book 'In the year of our Lord's Incarnation 849 Alfred King of the Anglo-Saxons was born'. The authors of *Vitae* in the Dark Ages rarely gave the date of their subject's birth. I believe the Astronomer may be the first to supply an A.D. date. Asser seems to have been the first to *begin* his life with the year of our Lord in which his subject was born: here, when he seems banal, he is original.

Something may be gleaned by setting Asser's book beside other Carolingian works: in particular the collection of stories about Charlemagne produced by a monk of St Gall, Notker in about 884; Ermoul's poem in praise of Louis the Pious (827); and Abbo's, written in 897 and describing the siege of Paris by the Danes some ten years earlier.[30]

There are scholarly minds to whom Notker does not endear himself: he is late, discursive, demonstrably unreliable, intensely amusing. Still, his unique collection of stories reveals much about what Franks of Asser's day could think they knew about a previous generation; and about the nature of the anecdotes in which such information was transmitted. The attraction of comparable tales for Asser, the extent to which he could not altogether emulate the tight-fisted control of Einhard, is indicated by his including two such. One is of Eadburh, Offa's daughter and Beorhtric's queen; her overbearingness, her accidental poisoning of her spouse, her encounter with Charlemagne; her bad end, begging her bread in Pavia.[31] The other tells how two monks of Athelney nearly succeeded in murdering their abbot.[32] Asser cannot make these tales more than tangentially relevant to his main theme; but he nevertheless allows them a large share, together about a fourteenth, of his little book — it is only some 12,000 words long. Why? One may reasonably suppose that the air was full of arresting stories, not least of the scandalous stories, which normal historical genres could not accommodate. Notker, most enterprising, found a means of recording some of these; Asser succumbed to the temptation to bodge in two (of different kinds).

What such poems as those of Ermoul and Abbo provide is eloquently described and richly detailed descriptions of episodes of the deepest interest to a warrior aristocracy: episodes of war and diplomacy. Such a book as Einhard's provided no space at all for details of heroic deeds of individuals; and no more than the most summary account of diplomatic activity. It was to verse that one had to turn to learn of such feats as Ebles's spitting seven Danes on his spear and suggesting they be taken to the kitchen,[33] or of the sumptuous enjoyments of such a diplomatic occasion as Harold of Denmark's visit to Louis the Pious.[34]

A most attractive feature of Ermoul's account of this visit is a marvellous description of a great hunt in which the Danes participated.[35] Alfred would have enjoyed such a description; hunting was one of his passions, 'incomparabilis omnibus peritia et felicitate in illa arte'.[36] Doubtless it played a part in his diplomatic entertainments as it did in those of Louis and Charlemagne. Asser says nothing at all about such entertainments, nor indeed anything about Alfred's relations with secular powers outside Britain, except in one sentence which seems to say that he was in almost daily intercourse with rulers from the Tyrrhenian Sea to the furthest shores of Ireland.[37] It may well be that in England as in Gaul the description of heroic deeds and of splendours of particular diplomatic occasions was the concern not so much for prose as for verse, in the vernacular or in Latin. Poems such as those on the battles of Brunanburh and (especially) Maldon supplied heroic detail. Until Dr Lapidge questioned, powerfully, the hitherto-accepted view that William of Malmesbury's account of Athelstan derived from a contemporary poem, one would have said that this poem was very much a case in point, for William's account is extensively concerned with foreign relations, not least with the exceedingly grand marriages made by Athelstan's sisters.[38] But it seems unquestionable that Malmesbury did have one or more tenth-century sources for much of what he relates of Athelstan. They probably included the work, in contorted Latin, which he found 'in ... volumine vetusto', and not improbably this was a poem. (Dr Lapidge's argument is not that this source was not poetic, but rather that it is to be distinguished from the poem which Malmesbury quotes, so that we cannot tell whether it was prose or verse.) My suggestion that it was in verse is a suggestion, not an argument, for as an argument it would be circular. Still, if one asks why the early tenth-century annals of the *Chronicle* have nothing to say about so large and attractive a subject as the marriages of English princesses to some of the greatest men in the West, the answer may be: because such matters were dealt with elsewhere, and in verse. The account by 'Florence of Worcester' of Edgar's being rowed on the Dee by subject kings, a grand diplomatic occasion if ever there was one, could have derived from a poem.[39]

In England vernacular poetry would have mattered more than Latin. Asser brings home very forcibly indeed the significance of *carmina Saxonica* in Alfred's education and in that of his children, and that such works were of lifelong interest to him.[40] It could be that *Beowulf* was one of these *carmina*.[41] It is a question whether they included poems on more recent history and events comparable to the Carolingian Latin verse, or to the *Battle of Maldon* of more than a century later. The possibility that they did so is strengthened by the fact that the Old High German *Ludwigslied* was a contemporary production: written between 881 when the battle it commemorates (like Maldon, one against Vikings) took place and the death of Louis III in 882.[42] Asser's repeated emphasis on the significance of *carmina* suggests the possibility that we should see his book, and the *Chronicle*, as works which were complemented by verse; and which may even have been in a sense residual. To consider such possibilities is to touch on a wide range of problems; not least those associated with origins of the *chansons de geste*. I shall not try to grapple with them here. (I would add one tentative suggestion. Perhaps the failure to use Sallust as a model in this period, though some of his works were known, may be because his style was suitable for works derived from, or replacing, those in verse; but not for those complementary to those in verse, as I am tentatively suggesting ninth-century royal annals and biographies to have been.)

So far I have been trying to explore Asser's work by setting it beside that of certain Carolingian authors. In seeking to face the question of its purpose more directly, there is the usual risk of seeking for the organised implementation of conscious purpose in circumstances where the author himself may have been confused or undetermined in intention. It is a risk easier to confess than to avoid.

Whatever Asser did for Alfred it was something for which Alfred found it very worthwhile to pay. Early in their relationship Alfred gave Asser a very precious silk robe, and a strong man's load of incense. And that, Asser emphasises, was only the beginning. Alfred was *profusus in largitate*. His gifts were 'daily' and 'innumerable' and included two monasteries with all their contents and property.[43] It may be that much about Alfred is to be explained by his wealth. Asser brings out this aspect of his power as no other source does, partly because, somewhat in the manner of Suetonius, he regards it as germane to his purpose to say something of his subject's activities as a builder and as a patron of the arts. So he tells of Alfred's *aurificae* and *artifices*, of his objects d'art *venerabiliora et pretiosiora* than those of his predecessors, his magnificent buildings in wood and stone, the large part of his income which he spent on *operatores*.[44] Providentially, the Alfred jewel survives to demonstrate some of the reality of the magnificence which Asser indicates. Alfred's successes may well have been in part attributable to his ability to pay *bellatores*,[45] to confer *multa et optima beneficia* such as he showered on Guthrum and his men when Guthrum *cum rege mansit* for twelve nights on the occasion of his baptism.[46] (Would not *Beowulf* have been a suitable poem for performance on that occasion?) Only such a king could afford scholars.[47] They came dear. We may recall Fichtenau's observation on Alcuin: 'Alcuin had crossed the English Channel with a single companion. In the end he was the lord of 20,000 human beings'.[48] Compare the Old English poem which Wulfsige put as a preface to his copy of the translation of Gregory's *Dialogues*: beginning with observations about sin, the saints, heaven and forgiveness: he ends by expressing the hope that he will come to rest with God; not only with God, also with his 'ring-giver' Alfred, 'the greatest treasure-giver of all the kings he has ever heard tell of, in recent times, or any earthly king he previously learned of'.[49] Wulfsige presents himself not only as a pious bishop, but also, like his successor at Sherborne, Asser, as a very grateful bishop.

How did Asser earn his rich rewards? In particular what was the function of his life of Alfred? An idea about this, first put forward in 1957 by Dr Schütt, powerfully reinforced and developed in 1971 by Dr Kirby, was two years ago accepted by Dr Keynes and Dr Lapidge in their weighty account of Asser.[50] It is this, that the life was written principally for the benefit of readers in Wales. The case for this, though complex, is not sufficient to prove that Asser had a Welsh audience *chiefly* in mind.

Undoubtedly there are passages explaining the author's own conduct which give a strong impression of being intended for a St David's audience; but the construction of the work is such that it is impossible to be confident that the chief intention of the whole may be deduced from the nature of a part.[51] Asser's inclusion of the Welsh equivalents of certain English place names may simply be indicative of an interest in etymology[52] and/or could reflect his having in mind a Welsh audience in South-West England or in his own household rather than in Wales.[53] His description of the Anglo-Saxons by such terms as *illa gens* etc. need do no more than indicate *his* Welshness rather than that of his intended audience. No matter how generously it is weighed, the evidence need mean no more than that Asser envisaged that part of his audience would be Welsh. His work is dedicated to Alfred, and can give a strong impression of being aimed at a specifically English audience, as in chapter 91, which seems concerned to drive home a lesson about the need to co-operate in Alfred's programme of fortification.

In arguing his case for Asser's writing for a Welsh audience, Dr Kirby lays stress on how he is likely to have acted as a link between Alfred and the rulers of Wales.[54] That Asser did have such a role is probable; but it was not his only role. He became bishop of Sherborne, possibly before he wrote his *Life*. This, as Dr Kirby has himself brought out, was by no means an obscure see, but that for all or most of the South Western peninsula.[55] Its importance is to an extent indicated by two, perhaps three, of Alfred's brothers being buried there.[56] Asser was not the only non-West Saxon whom Alfred appointed to his ecclesiastical office. John the Old Saxon was abbot of his monastery at Athelney. The Mercian Plegmund was made archbishop of Canterbury; and Grimbald was offered that see in 889 if his *Vita Prima* is to be believed.[57] Such appointments may indicate not only Alfred's need to find learned men where he could, but also the need to have reliable dependents in positions of power. Alfred may not have been without threats to his power — not least from the sons of his elder brothers. It is relevant to recall that a previous bishop of Sherborne, Eahlstan, had been a leader of the rebels against Aethelwulf in 856.[58] Alfred's employment of non-West Saxon ecclesiastics (and also his employment of non-West Saxon laymen) may have been, in part, an indication of his concern for internal security.[59]

So there is something to be said for treating Asser, at least hypothetically, not simply as a scholar and a Welshman, but as a key figure in a powerful, but possibly insecure, regime; a touch of Hincmar about him, perhaps. Should we see his *Life* as in some degree a contribution to Alfred's struggle for hegemony? The question is closely related to that of whether we should see the *Anglo-Saxon Chronicle* in a similar light. A warning has recently been issued by Dr Keynes and Dr

Lapidge on how we should judge the *Chronicle*. 'We should', they say, 'resist the temptation to regard it as a form of West Saxon dynastic propaganda'.[60] The temptation which Dr Keynes and Dr Lapidge manfully resist is one to which, in 1971, Professor R.H.C. Davis notoriously succumbed. In his article 'Alfred the Great: Propaganda and Truth'[61] he advances a variety of arguments for the *Chronicle*'s being in large measure propaganda; produced so close to the King that it is reasonable to assume that 'in a general sense he wrote it'.[62] He sees it as concerned to glorify, to an extent to magnify, Alfred's achievements; to create loyalty, 'to persuade his subjects of the necessity of accepting new and burdensome institutions'.[63] The strength of Professor Davis's case is great. The only apparent reason for some scholars' reluctance to accept that the *Chronicle* must have been produced close to the court is deference to the *auctoritas* of the late Sir Frank Stenton.[64] Professor Davis's case on the aims of the *Chronicle* is not one which can, in the main, be proved categorically; in so far as such proof would require objective sources (or at least sources from a different milieu) to set beside the *Chronicle*; and these we do not have. But the lack of such sources equally handicaps those seeking to support the opposite case: indeed it handicaps them more; for *prima facie* the *Chronicle* does appear to be Alfredian propaganda, to the extent that the *onus probandi* would seem to lie principally upon those who hold that it was not.

Asser and the *Chronicle* are intimately related, almost Siamese twins. He draws upon it very largely; and to an extent his purposes and those of its author(s) must coincide. A particularly important instance of the relationship between the two sources is in the treatment of that odd episode, Alfred's visit (or alleged visit) to Rome as a small child in 853. Asser says that on that visit Pope Leo anointed Alfred as King (*Leo papa...Alfredum...unxit in regem*). He is following the A version of the *Chronicle*. But his testimony 'is of crucial importance because he translates the Anglo-Saxon *gehalgode* by the unequivocal *unxit*'.[65] Dr Nelson has argued powerfully that whatever happened to the infant Alfred at Rome it was not a royal anointing. A fragment of a letter from Leo IV had appeared to give some degree of confirmation to the story; but she shows that it may very well be an eleventh century forgery. It could have suited Alfred to have it believed that he had been regally anointed by a pope. It follows that if the *Chronicle* is essentially a court Chronicle, then what we have here in the A version (in which alone it appears) and (by derivation) in Asser is a false story purveyed in Alfred's interest and with his knowledge: as Dr Nelson suggests 'deliberate falsification'.[66]

Professor Davis and Dr Nelson at the very least strengthen the obvious case for treating Asser as above all an encomiast. The plainest of Asser's messages is that of the perfection of Alfred; of course, no such medieval writer as he stood in need of Disraeli's advice on how to handle a royal theme. Still, Asser was more intemperate in adulation than were his continental counterparts: Einhard very occasionally says something which he might be thought to suppose some would put to Charlemagne's discredit.[67] True, Charlemagne was dead by the time Einhard wrote; but even Thegan, Asser's nearest counterpart, writing of the living Louis, says that he was perhaps too devoted to psalm-singing and to study.[68] Asser's adultion of Alfred was unrelenting, and it echoes through the text-books yet.

To golden deference he added iron discretion. Not one word do Asser or the *Chronicle* say about the internal dynastic politics of Wessex during Alfred's reign. Alfred had succeeded as a youngest son, with sons of his brothers living; and he ruled Wessex as an undivided kingdom though its recent tradition had been of a degree of division. The possibility, indeed likelihood, that these circumstances caused stress, is indicated by what happened upon Alfred's death, when his nephew sought to oust his son from the throne.[69] It would be dangerous in the extreme to assume from the silence of our narrative sources that Alfred's reign was so extraordinary as to contain no rebellion or intrigue of any kind (indeed, a charter provides evidence for the rebellion of one ealdorman[70]). There is a chasm in the evidence, often ignored. There is no period of Carolingian history on which annalists and biographers are so reticent about internal affairs as Asser and the *Chronicle* are about those of Alfred's reign.

That this discretion derives from Asser's attitude to Alfred rather than from his attitude to the past or to the West Saxon house in general is indicated by his providing detail of a more revealing kind (and detail which the *Chronicle* does not provide) in relation to the rebellion against Aethelwulf in 856 and the battle of Ashdown in 871. It is not hard to see why he does this; in both cases the information provided is such as to discredit one of Alfred's brothers.[71] The superiority of Alfred to his brothers is stressed not only by inference but directly: it is in this form that the difficulties over the succession come through into Asser.

A second lesson Asser teaches is military; a long chapter (91) is devoted to the folly and grim fate of those who did not undertake fortification as the king ordered. Another, and recurrent, theme is that of unity, expressed in the repeated use of the neologism *Angulsaxones* to describe the peoples over whom Alfred ruled, a term which had no English equivalent in the *Chronicle,* and for Asser no territorial equivalent (he always says *Saxonia et Mercia*, never *Anglia*, or *Angulsaxonia*). (An element absent from Asser, and from the *Chronicle,* is any of the adulation of the English such as Frankish writers provided for the Franks: there is nothing to·correspond to that glorying in the role of successful predator which leads Einhard to quote his Greek proverb to the effect that if one has the Frank as a friend and it means that one does not have him as a neighbour,[72] Ermoul to revel in the rapine and destruction of the Franks in Catalonia.[73])

Much of what Asser says about Alfred is in a vein of pious panegyric, which does not require to be swallowed whole. It would be absurd to make so trite an observation, were it not that it is accepted, widely if surprisingly, that his account of Alfred's character and purposes must be essentially accurate. Alfred may, however, have been more like his Danish enemies than the court sources for his reign generally allow. Asser may give a hint of this when he says that in 885, Alfred sailed to East Anglia with his fleet, full of *bellatores, praedandi causa*.[74] We know that on occasion, under pressure of necessity, he would plunder pagan and Christian alike.[75] Asser writes with the zeal of the well-rewarded. Perhaps not all took the same view. Part of Alfred's success and that of his son may well have depended on the annexation of monastic lands.[76] At Abingdon in the twelfth century it was believed that 'Aelfredus...villam...quae vulgari onomare Abbandun dicitur, cum omnibus suis adjectivis, a praedicto coenobio abstraxit; victori Domino impares pro victoria quae functus est reddente taliones'.[77] 'Quasi Judas inter XII' commented a later Abingdon monk.[78]

It helps, in resisting Asser's unction, to consider Carolingian accounts of pious kings. For example, Notker on Louis the German. Louis was, Notker says, indefatigable as a protector of the servants of Christianity, and in study of the scriptures; zealous in prayer, rigorous in fasting, he seemed to have the Lord always before his eyes. Hard on bad clerks, kind to good ones, he was very good at cheering people up; a glance from him sufficed to quell any impropriety.[79] One can hardly mistake the similarity of Asser's vein. A principal reason why what Asser says has been widely accepted is that the quasi-autobiographical passages in the Alfredian translations seem to bear out much of what he says. Dr Kirby has been virtually alone in urging caution here.[80] The actual fact that the translations were made *does* tell one that something very remarkable was happening at his court. But, as Dr Kirby rightly pointed out, the extent of Alfred's real participation in translation is a matter for speculation, and there is no reason for taking all that the king says, or is made to say, as *ipso facto* true. The Alfred some people seem to know — know and love, indeed, — may be in some measure a ghost, the creation of his clerical courtiers.

If Asser is sterotyping Alfred, and one can be virtually certain that he is, it is important that the exemplar or exemplars are not antique. There is nothing remotely resembling Einhard's Augustan rendering of

Charlemagne. This reflects a strong contrast between the works produced at Alfred's court, and many of those from the Carolingian world. The former entirely lack the classicising vein prominent in many of the latter. When Ermoul asks Christ to give him the gifts of David so that he may do justice to Caesar, as when the Astronomer compares Charlemagne to Pompey and Hannibal, these authors strike notes never struck by those who wrote for Alfred.[81]

Asser does not make Alfred sound in the least like a Roman emperor; he makes him sound not unlike a kind of saint; and perhaps he makes him sound most of all like a Pope, Gregory the Great.[82] There is of course no difficulty in demonstrating the influence of Gregory's writings. It is very likely that Asser had read Bede's account of Gregory in Book I of the *Ecclesiastical History*. In several important respects he does indeed make his Alfred sound like a lay version of Gregory: in his account of Alfred's struggle with illness, of his seeking at every opportunity the consolation of spiritual discussion with a circle of those qualified to provide it, of his attitude towards *sapientia*, of his concern for the poor and for justice.[83] One cannot be sure that Asser intends such a comparison. But note that a ruler could be compared to a saint even when he was not being presented *as* a saint. Notker says that Louis the German was like St Ambrose, except, he says, in certain matters without which life cannot go on, namely the use of weapons and marriage; indeed, he adds, Louis was in some ways rather *better* that St Ambrose.[84] It is noticeable that Asser is concerned to emphasis Alfred's anxiety to remain chaste, something which was among the lesser of Einhard's, or Charlemagne's, concerns.[85]

Asser is very hard to approach, not least because to understand him we need to understand the milieu in which he wrote; but he himself provides a large part of the evidence for the nature of that milieu. This problem of circularity is felt most acutely when such a source is presenting a stereotype; for a world in which stereotypes were present was one in which they could be imitated. Einhard's statement that Charlemagne seldom had more than three drinks at a meal faces us with an impasse characteristic of such sources. Suetonius says just the same thing of Augustus' drinking habits. Was Einhard imitating Suetonius, or was Charlemagne imitating Augustus, of whose habits he could have learned, e.g. from Einhard?[86]

It is in cramping awareness of such difficulties that one tries to speculate about the intended audience for Asser.[87] Unless one assumes that his book's purposes are largely to be summed up in terms of Alfred's and Asser's Welsh intentions then, I would suggest, the prime intended audience was the king himself. When a richly endowed author produces a work dedicated to his royal *dominus*, and presents him in a uniformly and intensely favourable light, is it not likely that it is for the royal eye that it is intended? Alfred's monastic foundations at Athelney and Shaftesbury could have been willing recipients of Asser's work. Many of the monks at Athelney were Franks; they would value a work containing a Latin version of the *Chronicle*; and indeed there are some grounds for supposing that they may have been involved in the composition of the *Chronicle*.[88] Shaftesbury was Alfred's daughter's nunnery; it is likely that in England, as in Germany, royal women were particularly interested in history and there is a scrap of evidence to suggest the possibility of a manuscript having been copied there in about 1000 A.D.[89] Presumably there was, or was hoped to be, a wider audience: here questions arise about the nature and success of the Alfredian educational programmes. I will merely say that to the extent to which Alfred may have been seeking to mould an élite, and perhaps to make a new élite, Asser's account of the king could have made its contribution to purposes not all, necessarily, to be defined in terms of *sapientia*.

It would be wrong to conclude without a tribute to Asser. He is the most successful of Dark Age historians. In this sense: no other has ensured that his view of his hero remains so widely accepted as his of Alfred is.[90] Well did he earn his incense: and well might it have been incense.

NOTES

1. Ed. W.H. Stevenson, *Asser's Life of King Alfred* (new impression with an article on recent work by D. Whitelock, Oxford, 1959). All references to Asser below are to this edition. The most recent translation, with a valuable commentary, is that by S. Keynes and M. Lapidge, *Alfred the Great. Asser's Life of King Alfred and other Contemporary Sources* (Harmondsworth, 1983).
2. For the construction of the work see esp. M. Schütt, 'The Literary Form of Asser's *Vita Alfredi*', *EHR*, 62 (1957), pp. 209–20 (Dr Schütt is particularly interesting on Asser's handling of problems of genre, cf. pp. 117–20 below), and D.P. Kirby, 'Asser and his Life of King Alfred', *Studia Celtica*, 6 (1971), pp. 12–35.
3. V.H. Galbraith, *An Introduction to the Study of History* (1964), p. 121.
4. See Keynes and Lapidge (n. 1 above), pp. 50–51 for a summary of the arguments of Whitelock and others vindicating Asser's authenticity. Neither Galbraith, nor his critics, appear to have noticed the interesting (if erroneous) arguments of J.W. Adamson, 'Who was "Asser"?, *The Illiterate Anglo-Saxon* (Cambridge, 1946), pp. 21–37) which anticipate some of Galbraith's.
5. Asser, cc. 94, 96.
6. J.M. Wallace-Hadrill, 'The Franks and the English in the Ninth Century: Some Common Historical Interests', *Early Medieval History* (Oxford, 1975), pp. 201–16, and D. Bullough, 'The Educational Tradition in England from Alfred to Aelfric: Teaching *Utriusque Linguae*', *Settimane di studio del centro italiano di studi sull'alto medioevo*, 19 (1972), pp. 453–94; a most important contribution.

7. For recent discussion of some of what remains, M. Lapidge, 'Some Latin Poems as Evidence for the Reign of King Athelstan', *ASE* 9 (1981), pp. 61–98.

8. For example the Frankish annals are methodically concerned with the movements of the ruler as those of the English *Chronicle* are not.

9. For the Carolingian background to Asser see especially Stevenson pp. 1xxxi–1xxxii (pp. xciii–xciv, 208–6 for the possibility of his having studied in Francia). Cf. J. Bateley, 'Grimbald of St Bertin's', *Medium Aevum* 35 (1966), pp. 1–10, and esp. Bullough (n. 6 above). For John the Old Saxon, Lapidge (n. 7 above). Dr Kirby also lays stress on the likelihood of Frankish influence on Asser, and in Wales: *op.cit.* (n. 2 above), p. 34 and n.

10. Chap. 73, cf. Stevenson p. lxxxi and n. 1. See Galbraith (n. 3 above), pp. 105–8.

11. B. Smalley, *Historians in the Middle Ages* (1974), p. 71.

12. Ed. L. Halphen, *Éginhard: Vie de Charlemagne* (3rd edn, Paris 1947), p. xi.

13. A. Wallace-Hadrill, *Suetonius* (1983), p. 13.

14. *Cc.* 99–102.

15. Ed. Halphen, pp. 94–103.

16. Though Alfred's will (F.H. Harmer, *Select English Historical Documents of the Ninth and Tenth Centuries* (Cambridge, 1914), pp. 15–19) dates from between 873 and 888 and its contents may have been publicly known.

17. Ed. Halphen, p. 94. For Charlemagne's death Einhard gives the year of the emperor's life, his regnal year, the day, the very hour: but not the A.D. year (*ibid.* p. 86)

18. Ed. Halphen, p. 20.

19. *Ibid. Cc.* 9 and 13. Dr Schütt (n.2 above), pp. 219–20, brings out important contrasts between Asser and Einhard.

20. I have used the texts printed by R. Rau, *Quellen zur Karolingischen Reichesgeschichte* (Darmstadt, 1974), i. pp. 216–53 (Thegan); 258–381 (the 'Astronomer').

21. *Op.cit.* (n. 6 above), pp. 455, n. 2.

22. Ed. G. Pertz, *MGH, SS* ii (Hanover, 1839), p. 589.

23. Ed. Rau, pp. 226–30, 24–42.

24. Ed. Rau, pp. 274–6, 280, 284–8.

25. Ed. Rau, pp. 262, 288.

26. Ed. Rau, p. 216.

27. *Loc. cit..* The A.D. date in Charlemagne's will could similarly have been used as a key to determine A.D. dates for other events mentioned by Einhard, cf. p. 117, n. 17 above.

28. *Op. cit.* (n. 11 above), p. 21.

29. Ed. Halphen, p. xvii and n.

30. R. Rau, *Quellen zur Karolingischen Reich* (Darmstadt, 1975), iii, 322–47; H. Waquet, ed., *Abon. Le Siège de Paris par les Normands* (Paris, 1942); E. Faral, ed., *Ermold le Noir. Poème sur Louis le Pieux et Lettres au Roi Pepin* (Paris, 1932). For Carolingian poetry in general now see, P. Godman, *Poetry of the Carolingian Renaissance* (1985).

31. *Cc.* 14, 15. Asser's report of the dialogue with Charlemagne (*c.* 15) is in a similar vein to Notker's reports of similar dialogues with the emperor, e.g. ed. Rau, pp. 328–30, 336–8, 340, 346.

32. *Cc.* 95–97.

33. Ed. Waquet, pp. 22–23. The evidence to which Professor Bullough draws attention (*op. cit.* n. 6 above, p. 468, n. 32) that a copy of Abbo's poem was in England in the late tenth-century suggests the possibility of unexplored relationships between Continental and English historical verse.

34. Ed. Faral, pp. 167–91. Such scenes *do* appear in Notker, e.g. ed. Rau, pp. 380–94. It is characteristic of Notker that he is extensively concerned with matters which would not receive in *annales, gesta,* or *vitae* the treatment he gives them.

35. Ed. Faral, pp. 180–84.

36. P. 20.
37. Asser also mentions contacts with the Pope and with the Patriarch of Jerusalem, *cc.* 86, 91. The *Chronicle* says nothing of diplomatic contacts in Alfred's reign other than with Rome and India.
38. *Op. cit.* (n. 7 above), pp. 62–71.
39. Ed. B. Thorpe, *Chronicon ex Chronicis* (2 vols., 1848–9), i, pp. 142–3.
40. Vernacular poetry was important to Alfred and his children, *cc.* 23, 76, 75.
41. For possible West Saxon connections of *Beowulf*, and in particular between its early lines and the West Saxon royal genealogy as drawn up in Alfred's reign, M. Lapidge, '"*Beowulf*", Aldhelm, the "Liber Monstrorum" and Wessex', *Studi Medievali*, 3rd ser. 23 (1982), pp. 151–91 and A.C. Murray, 'Beowulf, the Danish Invasions and the Royal Genealogy', in *The Dating of Beowulf*, ed. C. Chase (Toronto etc., 1981), pp. 101–12.
42. J.K. Bostock, *A Handbook on Old High German Literature* (2nd ed., revised by K.C. King and D.R. McLintock, Oxford, 1976), p. 239–46.
43. *C.* 81.
44. *Cc.* 76 (p. 59), 91 (p. 77), 101 (p. 87). Of course the impression of wealth which Asser gives is not quantifiable. Our only figures on Alfred's movable resources come from his will (872 X 888 cf. p. 117 n. 16 above). In this he leaves sums amounting to 1800 pounds of silver and probably not less than 1300 mancuses. These are small compared to those of which later Anglo-Saxon rulers disposed; though Alfred intimates that he believed he possessed more money than he was leaving.
45. *C.* 100 (p. 86): '...cuius primam divisionis partem suis bellatoribus annualiter largiebatur, item suis ministris nobilibus...'.
46. *C.* 56 (p. 47).
47. It is interesting that two of Alfred's scholarly bishops, Werferth and Plegmund, seem to have received important (and adjacent) estates in London in connection with the Alfredian reconstruction there: T. Dyson and J. Schofield, 'Saxon London', in *Anglo-Saxon Towns in Southern England*, ed. J. Haslam (Chichester, 1984), pp. 296–7.
48. H. Fichtenau, *The Carolingian Empire* (Oxford, 1957), p. 86.
49. D. Yerkes, 'The Full Text of the Metrical Preface to Waerferth's Translation of Gregory', *Speculum* 55 (1980), pp. 505–13. I have used the translation by Keynes and Lapidge, pp. 187–8.
50. Schütt, *op. cit.* (n. 2 above), p. 210; Kirby, *op. cit.* (n. 2 above), pp. 12–35; Keynes and Lapidge, *op. cit.* (n. 1 above). pp. 41, 56.
51. E.g. one does not have to go all the way with Dr Kirby's analysis to recognise that the work as we have it may draw on other compositions by the same author the aim of which was not necessarily the same.
52. Asser gives Latin equivalents for a number of English place-names (*cc.* 1, 3, 5, 30, 35, 37); but so does Bede, whom no one supposes to have been writing for a British audience: *Baedae Opera Historica*, ed. C. Plummer (2 vols., Oxford, 1896), i, pp. 179, 207, 282, 283. Similarly, Asser gives British equivalents of Anglo-Saxon names in a way which could indeed be suggestive of his having a Welsh audience in mind e.g. '...et Snotengaham adiit (quod Britannice "Tigguocbauc" interpretatur, Latine autem "speluncarum domus")' (*c.* 30, cf. Stevenson's remarks, pp. 1xxvi–vii). But comparable passages in Bede suggest the possibility of interest in toponymy for its own sake: e.g. '...civitatem Legionum, quae a gente Anglorum Legacaestir a Brettonum rectius Carlegion appellatur' (ed. Plummer, i, p. 84, cf. p. 303). (It is not certain that Asser knew Bede's work.) For an example of ninth-century etymological interest, Ermold, ed. Faral, *op. cit.*, p. 11, on the meaning of *Hludovicus*.

53. Stevenson, pp. lxxvi, 241, 249, 251, 262 argues that Asser probably derived his knowledge of certain river names in S.W. England from Celtic-speaking inhabitants. For the possibilities of there having been Britons living under English rule in Wessex: H.P.R. Finberg, *The Early Charters of Devon and Cornwall* (Leicester, 1963), pp. 26–8. Five memorial stones in Lady St. Mary Church, Wareham, the latest of which may be ninth-century, commemorate Britons, who must have been of some status: Royal Commission on Historical Monuments, *Dorset*, ii, (*South East*), pt. ii, pp. 310–12.

54. *Op. cit.*, pp. 16–20.

55. D.P. Kirby, 'Notes on the Saxon Bishops of Sherborne', *Proc. Dorset Natural History and Archaeological Soc.*, 87 (1966), pp. 213–22.

56. Ed. C. Plummer and J. Earle, *Two of the Saxon Chronicles Parallel* (2 vols., Oxford, 1899), i, pp. 67, 68, 73n. For the significance of Sherborne in relation to the centre of royal authority at Dorchester, L. Keen, 'The Towns of Dorset' in *Anglo-Saxon Towns...* (n. 47 above), pp. 207–10 and esp. 230–31.

57. As P. Grierson suggests very possibly it should be: 'Grimbald of St Bertin's', *EHR*, 55 (1940), pp. 529–61, esp. p. 550.

58. C. 12 (p. 9). Mr A. Martins pointed this out to me. Ealhstan seems to have been important to Egbert and it is noteworthy that he appeared in at least two battles. Heahmund, bishop of Sherborne, was killed in battle in 871: Kirby, *op. cit.* (n. 55 above), pp. 213, 217–9.

59. It was not, presumably, from simple generosity that Alfred offered such rewards that 'franci autem multi, Frisones, Galli, pagani, Britones, et Scotti, Armorici sponte se suo dominio subdiderant'; and note that their rewards included not only *pecunia*, but also *potestas*: *c.* 76 (p. 60), cf. *c.* 77 (p. 62). Some at least of the *Frisones* were in Alfred's military service: that three of the five men (plainly of some consequence) killed in opposing the Danes in 896 were Frisians suggests that Alfred may have employed considerable Frisian forces: *Two of the Saxon Chronicles* (n. 56 above), i, p. 91.

60. *Op. cit.* (n. 1 above), p. 40.

61. *History*, 56 (1971), pp. 169–82.

62. P. 177. To the extent that Professor Davis's case rested on 'the strong resemblance between its (sc. the *Chronicle*'s) phraseology and that of King Alfred's translation of Orosius' (*loc.cit.*); it is weakened by demonstrations that it is unlikely that the O.E. Orosius is by the same hand as other translations attributed to Alfred: J.M. Bateley, 'King Alfred and the Old English translation of Orosius', *Anglia*, 88 (1970), pp. 433–60; E.M. Liggins, 'The Authorship of the Old English Orosius', *Anglia*, 88 (1970), pp. 289–322.

63. P. 182.

64. F.M. Stenton, 'The South-Western Element in the Old English Chronicle', *Preparatory to Anglo-Saxon England*, ed. D.M. Stenton (Oxford, 1970), pp. 106–15.

65. J.L. Nelson, 'The Problem of King Alfred's Royal Anointing', *JEH* 18 (1967), p. 155.

66. *Ibid.*, p. 158.

67. P. 56, the emperor's *concubinae*; p. 64 his undue tolerance of the cruelty of his wife; pp. 80–82 his attempted revision of laws producing 'pauca capitula et ea imperfecta'.

68. Ed. Rau, p. 288. The Astronomer gives a brisk description of how Louis the Pious was rebuked by Charlemagne for parsimony, ed. Rau, p. 268; and his account of how Louis did not follow advice he was given partly[?] to go to his father as he approached death 'ne forte per hoc patrem suspectum redderet' (ed. Rau, p. 286) (pp. 342–3) considers motive in a manner unparalleled in Asser's account of Alfred.

69. *Two of the Saxon Chronicles...* (n. 56 above), pp. 91–2.

70. W. de Gray Birch, *Cartularium Saxonicum* (3 vols. 1883–93), ii, no. 595, cf. Davis, *op. cit.* (n. 61 above), p. 180.

71. Aethelbald as a rebel against his father (Chap. 12, 13); in his account of Ashdown (Chap. 37–39) Asser describes how Ethelred would not lead his troops into action until he had finished hearing mass; although he says 'Quae regis Christiani fides multum apud Dominum valuit, sicut in sequentibus apertius declarabitur' (p. 29), nevertheless brings out the importance of Alfred's having attacked, like a boar *viriliter*, while his brother was still at his devotions (*loc.cit.*).
72. Ed. Halphen, p. 50.
73. Ed. Faral, p. 14., cf. the complacency with which the Astronomer describes how Louis the Pious dealt with the Gascons: 'uno...comprehenso atque adpenso, reliquis paene omnibus uxores aut filii sunt erupti'.
74. *C.* 67 (s.a. 884). Asser is here following a version of the *Chronicle*, one cannot tell quite how closely. The surviving versions do not bring out, as he does, that plunder was the purpose of the raid, though they do indicate that plunder has been secured. Ed. Plummer and Earle (n. 56 above), i, p. 78 '*þa hie þa ham weard wendon mid þaere herehype*' (Parker Chron.)
75. *C.* 53.
76. As is shown in the important article by R. Fleming, 'Monastic Lands and England's Defence in the Viking Age', *EHR*, 100 (1985), pp. 247–61.
77. *Chronicon Monasterii de Abingdon*, i, ed. J. Stevenson (Rolls Series, 1858), p. 50n.
78. *Ibid.*, p. 50. For the dates of Abingdon chronicles, F.M. Stenton, *The Early History of the Abingdon* (Reading, 1913), pp. 1–11.
79. Ed. Rau, pp. 396–8.
80. *Op. cit.* (n. 2 above), p. 34.
81. Ed. Faral, p.1; ed. Rau, p. 262.
82. I owe the suggestion to Miss A.E. Redgate. That Gregory's works were regarded as providing salutary advice for secular rulers is plain from, e.g., Hincmar's *De Cavendis...*: J. Devisse, *Hincmar, archeveque de Rheims 845–862* (3 vols., Paris, 1975–6), pp. 679–83.
83. Cf. *Baedae Opera Historica* (n. 52 above), pp. 73–7.
84. Ed. Rau, pp. 394–6.
85. Cf. p. 125, n. 67, 68 above.
86. E.K. Rand, 'On the History of the De Vita Caesarum of Suetonius in the Early Middle Ages', *Harvard Studies in Classical Philology*, 37 (1926), p. 45. His suggestion that Charlemagne may have sought an elephant from Haroun al Raschid because he believed, thanks to the *Historia Augusta*, that Aurelian had received such a beast from Persia seems extreme.
87. The assessment of Asser's purposes would be easier did we have a preface to his work. He may well have written one: prefaces could easily get lost; Einhard's preface is lacking from all manuscripts of group A: ed. Halphen, p. xv.
88. For the large Frankish element in the community at Athelney, see p. 116, n. 5 above. The grounds for considering seriously the possibility of an Athelney involvement in the composition of the *Chronicle* are as follows. First, in so far as the *Chronicle* is closely connected with the king and his aspirations, association with the monastery he founded, and one which he patronised generously, would be appropriate. Second, such a provenance would explain the 'Somerset' element which Stenton emphasised (above, n. 64). Third, that the Athelney community was largely Frankish could account for the very strong interest in Frankish affairs displayed in the *Chronicle*; for the decade 881–90 more words are devoted to Frankish information than to English; and such information is supplied for every year but two. It might be contended that the very military character of the *Chronicle* excludes the possibility of a monastic milieu for its composition. But Asser suggests that its abbot, John, was a man of some military knowledge (*c.* 97) 'ut audivimus de eo a quibusdam referentibus, bellicosae artis non

expers, si in meliori disciplina non studeret'. In the late ninth-century the avocations of abbot and soldier were not necessarily separate. Compare Abbo's account of the military activities of abbot Ebble (ed. Waquet, pp. 23–4, 79–80). It may be relevant here that Athelney was part of an elaborately fortified complex, M. Aston, 'The Towns of Somerset', in *Anglo-Saxon Towns...* (n. 47 above), pp. 183–5.
89. J. Campbell, 'England, France, Flanders and Germany: Some Comparisons and Connections', in *Ethelred the Unready : Papers From the Millenary Conference* (Oxford, 1978), p. 266, n. 22.
90. The extreme case of Alfredolatry is that of E.A. Freeman, *The Norman Conquest,* i (3rd ed., Oxford 1877), p. 49: 'Aelfred ... is *the most perfect character in history*' (my italics). I owe the reference and useful observations on this paper to Dr R.A. Fletcher. Other important observations and corrections I owe to Professor K.J. Leyser. I am grateful to both and to Professor R. H. C. Davis; none of these scholars is responsible for my errors.

APPENDIX: 'INCONSISTENCIES' IN ASSER

In his article of 1971 (n. 2 above) Dr Kirby argues that Asser's work is an 'imperfect fusion' of a series of four compositions written for despatch to Wales at successive dates between *c.* 885 and *c.* 894. His case rests largely on the recognition of elements of redundancy or inconsistency in the text (*loc.cit.,* pp. 13–15). It is contended below that the passages in question do not (with one possible exception) bear the interpretation put on them. Dr Kirby fairly says: 'As with much internal criticism the threads in this analysis of the life may occasionally have seemed slender and the arguments intuitive' but emphasises, reasonably, that, in such an analysis as his, the cumulative force of instances which are individually slight may be great. In maintaining that, nevertheless, his instances do not sustain his case, I would by no means wish to impugn the general value of his close analysis of the text; or of the many important observations he makes in an article which is one of the two most significant contributions to Asser studies since 1904. The passages to which Dr Kirby draws attention are as follows:

1. Chapter 91 contains 'a brief statement about the King's illness but no sign whatsoever that the author had any awareness that his readers would already have known all about this illness in view of the exhaustive treatment of the subject in chapter 74' (Kirby, p. 13). But the passage in question is part of a general acount of Alfred's tribulations and triumphs. It has the quality of a peroration and summary recapitulation on the King's illness is appropriate here.

2. It is similarly difficult, for the same reason, to see anything untoward in the presence in Chapter 91 of two sentences on Alfred's wars. Dr Kirby says they are 'hardly necessary' (p. 13) in view of account of Danish attacks provided earlier. The question is not one of necessity, however, but rather of appropriateness.

3. The same point is made in relation to the reference to Danish attacks in Chapter 93. It comes as part of Asser's account of possible reasons for monastic decline '...nescio quare, aut pro alienigarum infestationibus, qui saepissime terra

marique hostiliter irrumperet, aut etiam pro nimia illius gentis in omni genere divitiarum abundantia' etc. (11. 11–14). That the reader had already been provided with much detail on Danish assaults does not make this passage redundant in any but a most formal sense.

4. That John the Old Saxon is mentioned (Kirby, p. 14) in Chapter 94 with no reference to his having been (probably) already mentioned in Chapter 73 is indicative of conflation only if it is assumed that in such works second references to an individual invariably refer back to the first, which is not the case.

5. Dr Kirby detects a contradiction, again suggestive of conflation, in Chapter 42. 'Alfred is represented, on the one hand, as having been in a position to assume the kingship even before 871 because he was very warlike, and victorious in every battle, and on the other, as then reigning against his will, because he did not think it possible to withstand the assaults of the heathen, since, while his brothers were alive, he had experienced many disasters' (Kirby, p. 14). There is a contradiction here only if 'magna detrimenta multorum sustinuisset' is translated as 'experienced many disasters': Dr Keynes and Dr Lapidge's version (op.cit., p. 80) 'sustained great losses of many men' is better. I.e. Alfred feared his victories had been Pyrrhic.

6. Another contradiction is detected between Chapter 25 in which 'the king is still lamenting that he had never been taught in his younger years' while in Chapters 87 and 88 Asser describes how Alfred learned to read and translate Latin (Kirby, p. 14). These passages can convey different impressions of the King's attainments at the time of Asser's writing, which might be explained by 25's having been written before the events described in 87, 88. Such an explanation, though feasible, is not necessary. All 25 need be saying is that Alfred regretted the educational opportunities he had missed through most of his life: the implication that his aspirations still remained entirely unfulfilled is not inevitable.

7. Dr Kirby detects another contradiction between the conclusion of Chapter 75 describing how 'the children of Alfred in the court school simply learn carefully psalms and Saxon books' and the main body of the chapter which 'provides a much more elaborate picture of the palace school where books in Latin as well as in English are read and there is emphasis also on writing as well as reading' (Kirby, p. 14). Asser is providing an account of Alfred's five children. Aethelflaed is married: Aethelgifu has become a nun. So, the implication is, three remain at home. Of these, Aethelweard, the youngest, is being educated, in company with other noble and non-noble children, in writing and in reading books 'utriusque linguae'. (l.16, cf. Bullough, as at n.6 above). The two elder children Edward and Aelfthryth are not being allowed to live idly but learn the psalms, and books in English, especially English poems. I.e. Asser is, interestingly, distinguishing between the kind of education Aethelweard was receiving and that which Edward and Aelfthryth were receiving. There is no contradiction.

8. Dr Kirby lays stress on the significance of Chapter 74 as evidence for Asser's conflating compositions written at different times. This chapter, largely concerned with Alfred's illnesses, is not pellucid. Dr Schütt (as at n.2, p. 214–5) has argued that, for all its difficulties, it shows neither confusion or contradiction, but tells a coherent tale. Dr Kirby will not have this, contending rather that we

have here a doublet, a chapter conflating the versions of a single story relating to the effect of prayer on Alfred's health: in the 'first version' he asked for an affliction from which he was suffering to be replaced by another but not such as leprosy or blindness. In the second he prayed for an illness which would curb his carnal desires but not incapacitate him for affairs of state. Dr Kirby argues that the 'first version' can be dated 888–9, because it describes 'how the illness – persisted till his fortieth year', the 'second version' to 893–4 because Asser says the illness had lasted until the King's 45th year. There is a snag here though. Asser does not say in the 'first version' that the illness persisted till Alfred's fortieth year but (Chapter 74, l.10) 'a vigesimo aetatis suae anno usque quadregesimum, *et eo amplius*' (my italics). Dr Kirby suggests that the crucial three words 'were probably added in a subsequent transcription of that sentence by Asser' (Kirby, p. 15). At this point his argument becomes circular; '...et eo amplius' is very damaging for him. In short, Asser is consistent in 74: Dr Schütt's case holds. Asser is describing, in an admittedly dislocated way ('praeposterato ordine', l.41), this sequence of events. (i) In youth Alfred prayed for a disease which would keep him chaste but leave him useful. His prayers were answered, probably by piles. (ii) At a later date he prayed for this disease to be replaced by another, less severe, but not such as leprosy or blindness. In fact he was cured. (iii) But another illness, more severe, seized him on his wedding day and continued to afflict him all his life. A trace of inconsistency could be argued in relation to the nature of the disease. Asser says that as a result of his first prayer Alfred contracted *ficus*. He then says (*c.* 74, l.61) that that which struck him from his wedding-day was *infestius*; but then he raises the possibility (line 15) that this was *ficus*. But this is only in the form 'alii ficum existimabant'.

INDEX